PENGUIN BOOKS
Edward III

Jonathan Sumption is a former history fellow of Magdalen College, Oxford. He is the author of *Pilgrimage* and *The Albigensian Crusade*, as well as the first four volumes in his celebrated history of the Hundred Years War, *Trial by Battle*, *Trial by Fire*, *Divided Houses* and *Cursed Kings*. He was awarded the 2009 Wolfson History Prize for *Divided Houses*.

JONATHAN SUMPTION

Edward III

A Heroic Failure

PENGUIN BOOKS

PENGUIN BOOKS

UK | USA | Canada | Ireland | Australia
India | New Zealand | South Africa

Penguin Books is part of the Penguin Random House group of companies whose
addresses can be found at global.penguinrandomhouse.com.

First published by Allen Lane 2016
First published in Penguin Books 2018

001

Copyright © Jonathan Sumption, 2016

The moral right of the author has been asserted

Set in 9.5/13.5 pt Sabon LT Std
Typeset by Jouve (UK), Milton Keynes
Printed and bound in Great Britain by Clays Ltd, Elcograf S.p.A.

ISBN: 978-0-141-98867-2

www.greenpenguin.co.uk

Contents

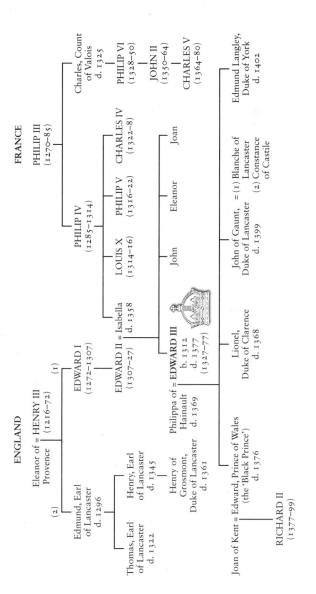

ENGLAND

Eleanor of = HENRY III
Provence (1216–72)

(1)

EDWARD I
(1272–1307)

EDWARD II = Isabella
(1307–27)   d. 1358

(2)

Edmund, Earl
of Lancaster
d. 1296

Thomas, Earl   Henry, Earl
of Lancaster   of Lancaster
d. 1322   d. 1345

Henry of
Grosmont,
Duke of Lancaster
d. 1361

FRANCE

PHILIP III
(1270–85)

PHILIP IV   Charles, Count
(1285–1314)   of Valois
                        d. 1325

LOUIS X   PHILIP V   CHARLES IV   PHILIP VI
(1314–16) (1316–22)   (1322–8)   (1328–50)

John   Eleanor   Joan   JOHN II
                                       (1350–64)

                                       CHARLES V
                                       (1364–80)

Philippa of = EDWARD III
Hainault   b. 1312
d. 1369   d. 1377
             (1327–77)

Lionel,   John of Gaunt, = (1) Blanche of Lancaster   Edmund Langley,
Duke of Clarence   Duke of Lancaster   (2) Constance   Duke of York
d. 1368   d. 1399   of Castile   d. 1402

Joan of Kent = Edward, Prince of Wales
              (the 'Black Prince')
              d. 1376

RICHARD II
(1377–99)

Edward III

I
Edward of Windsor
(1312–1330)

Edward III was King of England for fifty years. He was a paragon of kingship in the eyes of his contemporaries, the perfect king in those of later generations who have romanticized the institution of monarchy. He cut a fine figure. He led his armies in successful wars. He maintained a magnificent court. Venerated as the victor of Sluys and Crécy and the founder of the Order of the Garter, he was regarded with awe even by his enemies. Charles V of France, who was largely responsible for undoing his work, hung his portrait in his study. His great-grandson Henry V studied his campaigns and adopted his war aims. A century and a half after his death, Henry VIII, the last English king to toy with the idea of conquering France, consciously modelled himself on his famous ancestor. In the seventeenth century, the officials of Charles I copied documents from the public records to discover how he had managed his wars, while the parliamentary opposition held up Edward as a model to demonstrate the failures of their own age. King George III commissioned paintings from Benjamin West of the great occasions of Edward's reign. Prince Albert and Queen Victoria dressed up as Edward III and

Philippa of Hainault at fancy-dress balls. Yet for all the attention devoted to him in his lifetime and since, Edward III's personality is largely hidden behind the mask of kingship and a screen of uncritical adulation. Success is admirable in a king, but failure is compelling and usually better recorded. We know a great deal more about the personality of Edward's neurotic predecessor, Edward II, and of his vulnerable and unstable successor, Richard II, both of whom defied the conventions of their age and were deposed and murdered.

Edward was born at Windsor Castle on 13 November 1312. The country which he was destined to rule was one of the two principal nation-states of Europe, the other being France. But with around five or six million inhabitants, England had only about a third of the population of its neighbour. A large part of its territory was forest and some regions, especially in the west and north, were very thinly settled. London, the only English town to stand comparison with the major cities of continental Europe, probably had fewer than 50,000 inhabitants, as against about 200,000 for Paris, then the largest and richest city in Europe. England, however, was endowed with a precociously advanced system of government which made its kings powerful beyond anything warranted by its comparatively modest resources. Unlike France, which had developed as a nation by the gradual coalescence of ancient autonomous provinces, each with its own distinct political and cultural traditions, England had been conquered in the space of a few years in the eleventh century by the Norman kings, who had created a centralized, unitary state and settled it with a new, alien aristocracy. Three centuries later, Englishmen still had a highly developed notion of public authority. The king's authority extended to all places and all people. The common law was common to all England. The king's courts were open to all free men, and had exclusive jurisdiction over disputes about the possession of freehold land and the more serious crimes. The royal chancery, which operated as the king's secretariat, despatched orders daily to every corner of the land, while the Exchequer and the Treasury operated a system of revenue management more sophisticated than any in Europe. Almost alone among the representative assemblies of medieval Europe, the English parliament could bind the nation to legislation and grants of taxation. The contemporary French chronicler Jean Froissart, who knew England well, thought it the 'best governed land in the world'.[1]

It is one of the paradoxes of England's medieval history that in spite of its strong central institutions it was known mainly for its chronic political instability. In fact, the two things were connected. The fortunes of a powerful, centralized monarchy were inevitably dependent on the personality and political skills of the reigning monarch. Lacking the police powers of the modern state, even the most organized of medieval governments depended on the tacit assent of their leading subjects. In England, this meant some sixty baronial families, whose political power was based on their possession of large acreages of rural land and on their influence in the landowning communities of the counties. These men regarded themselves as the king's natural counsellors. Few of them were hungry for political power, and hardly any wanted to engage in the daily grind of government. But they resented exclusion more than they loved power. Their relationship with the crown was important to them. It was a major source of status and patronage. Twice in the previous century the baronage had intervened to take power out of the king's hands when the government had manifestly broken down, or when they conceived that power had already been taken out of his hands by others who were monopolizing his favours in their private interest.

The future Edward III was destined to inherit a poisonous legacy of internal upheaval and foreign war. His father, Edward II, had succeeded in 1307 to the imposing state built by the masterful Edward I. With it came the cumulative resentments which the old king had provoked over the three and a half abrasive decades of his reign. Edward II had scarcely been crowned before the baronage formally asserted that rebellion was a constitutional right. Their allegiance, they declared, bound them to the crown as an institution, but not to the person of any particular monarch. From this it followed that 'if, in his conduct of the Crown's business, the King is not guided by reason, his subjects are bound to guide him back to reason'.[2] Edward II was quite unequal to this challenge. The sensibilities of the twenty-first century would have found much to like in him: he was spontaneous, flamboyant, a hearty sportsman and a heavy drinker, with flashes of wit and no interest in conforming to contemporary stereotypes of kingship. But he was also completely devoid of political judgement. Worst of all, in the eyes of contemporaries, he formed strong attachments to a succession of favourites, whom he enriched and promoted beyond their rank. This not only united the baronage against him, but estranged him from the queen, Isabella of France, a daughter of the French king, Philip IV ('the Fair'). It led her to side with her husband's enemies and ultimately to assume the leadership of the opposition herself.

Edward of Windsor's childhood was overshadowed by the decade-long struggle for control of the government between his father and a baronial caucus led by his cousin Thomas, Earl of Lancaster. It culminated in the winter of 1321/2 in a savage civil war and Lancaster's bloody defeat at the Battle of Boroughbridge in March 1322. The earl was summarily put to death after the battle, and over the following weeks most of his former allies and followers were hunted down and executed as traitors. For the rest of his reign, while his son was growing to manhood, Edward II ruled as a solitary despot with the aid of the latest and closest of his favourites, his chamberlain, Hugh Despenser the Younger. Together with his father, Hugh the Elder (who became Earl of Winchester), Despenser gradually assumed complete direction of the government. The Despensers were able and hard-working, but they were also greedy and ruthless. They systematically excluded the higher nobility from the king's favour except for a small coterie of reliable allies. They brutally pursued the vendettas born of the civil war. And they despoiled their many enemies to build up great landed domains for themselves. It was an inherently unstable situation, which could only end in violence.

The Tuscan poet Dante Alighieri had a simple explanation for England's problematic status in fourteenth-century Europe. The difficulty, he thought, lay in their national character. The English were a proud and covetous people, ever eager for conquest and incapable of remaining peaceably within their own borders. Dante's opinion echoed the conventional sentiment of his day, which regarded England as a society to which violence and aggression came naturally. The true position was more complicated than that, and since England's relations with her neighbours were destined to dominate Edward III's life, it is necessary to say something about them. There were two major issues. The first was concerned with England's uncertain relations with her neighbours within the British Isles; and the second with her complicated relationship with her principal continental neighbour, France.

Although England was the dominant country of the British Isles, it occupied little more than half of their land mass. Its relations with the rest of Britain were characterized by aggressive colonization and periodic outbreaks of open war. Ireland was claimed by the kings of England as a hereditary lordship, having been thinly colonized by an Anglo-Norman aristocracy in the twelfth century. But it was not part of England. It had its own government and parliament, and it was never securely under English control. In Wales, the fertile southern and eastern regions had been colonized at about the same time and divided up into a large number of semi-autonomous territories controlled by the so-called lords of the march, most of whom were English barons. The rest of Wales had been conquered by

Edward I from its native princes between 1277 and 1294. It was held down by small English colonies established in the walled towns and castles, and by professional garrisons based in the mighty fortresses which Edward's engineers built along the north and west coasts. Wales remained a conquered land. It was not legally united with England or represented in Parliament until the sixteenth century.

It was, however, England's relations with Scotland and France that were destined to monopolize the attention of Edward III in the early years of his reign.

Situated, as its leaders proclaimed in 1320, 'at the uttermost ends of the earth',[3] Scotland, like Ireland and Wales, had been colonized by Norman migrants from England who had settled in the fertile southern and eastern lowlands in the twelfth century. But unlike Ireland and Wales, Scotland was an independent realm under its own dynasty. In 1290, however, the ancient line of the Scottish kings became extinct, and Edward I seized the opportunity to assert a claim to the overlordship of Scotland. In the following year, he entered Scotland with a large army and claimed the right to decide between the rival claimants to the Scottish succession. He set up a tribunal of 'auditors', which in 1292 awarded the Scottish crown to John Balliol, an English nobleman whose mother owned extensive lands in Scotland. But Edward I never intended to allow Balliol to succeed to the position of earlier kings of Scotland. He required Balliol to do homage to him, treated him as a subordinate princeling and in 1296 finally deposed him and sent him off to imprisonment in England while Scotland was reoccupied by Edward's armies. This brought him into collision with a large part of the Scottish nobility, led by the Bruce lords of Annandale, one of the great Anglo-Norman noble houses of Scotland, who had been Balliol's chief rivals as claimants to the Scottish throne.

In 1306, a decade after Balliol's deposition, Robert Bruce seized the Abbey of Scone, the traditional place of coronation of the Scottish kings. Here, he had himself crowned King of Scotland and embarked upon a twenty-year war against the English occupiers. He was fortunate in his timing. In July 1307, Edward I died at Burgh-on-Sands on the Solway Firth while leading a fresh army into Scotland to suppress the new rebellion. Between Edward's death and 1313, Bruce succeeded in extending his authority to almost all of Scotland and recovered every major English fortress in the country except three. Lacking his father's military reputation and distracted by the constitutional crisis in England, Edward II was compelled to stand by helplessly. In the autumn of 1313, he was forced into action by Robert Bruce's siege of Stirling Castle, the most important surviving English garrison in Scotland. Its governor agreed to surrender the castle unless it was relieved by Midsummer's Day 1314. On the day before the deadline expired, Edward II was approaching the beleaguered castle with a large English army when he was attacked by Bruce at Bannockburn. The English were defeated with terrible slaughter. Within five years, what was left of the English positions in Scotland had collapsed.

Hostility between England and France had more ancient origins. The root of the problem was the possession by the kings of England of extensive territories in France. In the twelfth century, these possessions had comprised about a third of the French kingdom, including almost all of its Atlantic provinces. But by the end of the thirteenth century all that remained of this empire was the duchy of Aquitaine, a vast and variegated province comprising the Atlantic coast from the mouth of the Charente to the Pyrenees and extending inland as far as Périgueux, Sarlat, Agen and Auch.

Aquitaine was never an English colony. Very few Englishmen were settled there. The seneschal, the king's chief representative in the duchy, was usually English, but otherwise the administration was largely in the hands of native Gascons. Its status was governed by the Treaty of Paris of 1259. The effect of this treaty was that the duchy was not an English possession but a personal possession of the English kings in their capacity as peers of France. This was also how the kings' English subjects viewed the matter. They had never overtly accepted any responsibility for Aquitaine, and throughout the thirteenth century had consistently refused to grant taxes to defend it. It was a serious weakness.

Another weakness was even more serious. In their capacity as dukes of Aquitaine, the English kings were amenable to the French king's laws and to the jurisdiction of his courts. This was becoming an increasingly irksome burden. In the first place, the kings of England were bound to do homage to the kings of France for their French territories. This involved a ritual of subordination, performed in person and in public, something which was not easy for men who were sovereigns in their own realm. Some of the political and legal obligations associated with this subordination were a major source of tension. In the course of the thirteenth century, the French monarchy had undergone a process of administrative and judicial centralization not unlike the one which had occurred rather earlier in England. This had greatly diminished the autonomy of France's ancient provinces and the independence of their territorial princes, including the English dukes of Aquitaine. In particular, the Gascon subjects of the King of England were entitled to challenge his decisions and those of his officers in the French royal courts, culminating in the final court of appeal in Paris, the Parlement. The intrusiveness of the French judges and officials tended to vary with the state of Anglo-French relations generally. But there had been a marked deterioration during the reign of Philip the Fair, who occupied the French throne between 1285 and 1314. Philip was a man of strong authoritarian instincts whose expansive notions of royal power were strikingly similar to those being pursued by Edward I at the same moment in the British Isles.

In 1293, Philip provoked a showdown with his rival. He ordered the English seneschal of Gascony to deliver up a number of Gascons accused of piracy in the Bay of Biscay for trial and punishment in France. They included most of the civic dignitaries of the city of Bayonne. The seneschal refused. Edward I was summoned to appear before the Parlement to answer for their contumacy. The following year, the court declared Edward to be in default and confiscated the duchy, which was occupied by French officials backed by French armies. At the same time, the French king made common cause with the Scots, concluding the original 'auld alliance' with them in 1295. The pope, Boniface VIII, a shrewd old Francophobe, could see what the French were about. He accused the Chancellor of France to his face of trying to drive the English dynasty out of France. 'Of course,' the chancellor replied with a smile.[4]

In fact, Edward I recovered Aquitaine, but only by a stroke of good fortune and shorn of some its outlying areas. In 1302, the towns of Flanders rose in rebellion against Philip the Fair and inflicted a shattering defeat on the French army at the Battle of Courtrai. Overstretched financially, and confronted by the threat of a war on two fronts at once, Philip restored the duchy to Edward I in the following year. But the incident left a bitter legacy. Edward I's officials drew much the same conclusion as Boniface VIII. It was intolerable that the kings of England should be sovereigns in their own realm and yet obliged to deal as subjects with the kings of France. If the current state of affairs continued, it would lead inevitably to the permanent loss of Aquitaine. The only alternative, they advised, was at some convenient moment to repudiate the treaties with France and renounce the English dynasty's status as vassal of the French kings.

These problems, quarrels with neighbours, constitutional challenges and internal disorder were destined to cast a dark shadow over England and over the young Edward of Windsor.

The lives of medieval children were notoriously fragile, and even royal princes were rarely noticed by contemporaries before they came of age. The childhood of Edward III has left hardly any trace in the sources. He was brought up in his own household with his younger brother, John, his two sisters and a small group of young noblemen. The household was dominated by various female servants under the supervision of officers nominated by the king, whose functions were mainly financial and administrative. We know their names, but little more. We know the titles of books that were presented to the young prince, but not whether he ever read them. At some stage, he must have been trained in the traditional accomplishments of a nobleman: riding, jousting and hunting, dancing and music, French and Latin letters, and the articles of the Christian faith. But we do not know how or by whom. Judging by the largesse which he poured on her in later life, the chief figure in Edward's early life was a woman called Margaret Daventry, a lady of modest rank who may have been his nursemaid, but of whom almost nothing is known. Edward's father was indulgent to the young prince, but distant. His mother, the lonely and unhappy Isabella of France, seems to have had very little to do with him until he was old enough to matter politically.

The young prince must gradually have become conscious of his father's political difficulties. In 1320, when he was seven years old, he received his first summons to attend Parliament, sitting among the lords, although his presence there must have been purely formal. He was with his father at York in 1322 in the aftermath of the Battle of Boroughbridge, when several of the king's opponents were butchered by his executioners in the castle ward. But it was not until Edward was thirteen years old that another crisis in England's relations with France propelled him into public affairs.

Edward II's marriage to a French princess in 1308 should have smoothed the course of diplomacy, and for a few years seems to have done so. But in the 1320s the couple fell out as a result of the king's relationship with Hugh Despenser the Younger. Isabella began to conspire with Despenser's many enemies. One of them was Roger Mortimer of Wigmore, a long-standing rival of Despenser's who had been imprisoned in the Tower of London awaiting execution, but managed to escape to France. Protected by Isabella's brother Charles IV, Mortimer assumed the leadership of a group of disaffected English exiles in Paris. In 1323 there was a major crisis in Anglo-French relations. The priory of Saint-Sardos in Gascony was the subject of current litigation in the Parlement in Paris and was under the protection of the French king's officers. A Gascon nobleman burned the place to the ground and hanged a French royal officer who was found there, almost certainly with the connivance of the English seneschal. The incident provoked another French invasion of Aquitaine. The whole of its territory was overrun apart from the coastal strip. In England, the Despensers responded by having Isabella arrested as an enemy alien. All her lands were confiscated and her household (most of which was French) was disbanded. In order to rescue his sister from her predicament, Charles IV proposed a fresh round of negotiations over Gascony and suggested that Edward II should appoint

Isabella as his ambassador. It was an unusual idea, but with some misgivings, Edward agreed. His wife left for France in March 1325.

Six months later, in September 1325, Edward of Windsor followed his mother across the Channel. His father, who was desperate to avoid doing homage to the French king in person, had hit upon the idea of transferring the duchy of Aquitaine to his heir and sending him to do homage in his place. Charles IV agreed to this proposal, probably at the suggestion of his sister, who saw an opportunity to extract her son from the Despensers' grip. The Despensers soon realized that they had made a serious mistake. Once Edward of Windsor was safely ensconced in his mother's household in Paris, Isabella refused to return to England or to send back her son. Instead, she set up with Roger Mortimer, who shortly became her lover. They began to build up support among prominent English soldiers and diplomats in France, including Edward II's brother the Earl of Kent, who was in command on the march of Gascony. It shortly became clear that the queen was planning nothing less than an armed invasion of England with a view to overthrowing her husband's government. Ever more strident missives arrived from Edward II in England addressed to both mother and son, demanding their return. Unless he complied, Edward wrote, the young man would 'feel his wrath all the days of his life'.[5] Isabella replied that she would not return while the Despensers remained in power and would not allow her son to go either. She needed the prince. He was her ticket to power.

Charles IV had connived at much of Isabella's scheming, but he was a strait-laced man who disapproved of his sister's liaison with Mortimer and drew the line at sponsoring an invasion of England mounted from his territory. So in August 1326, Isabella and her fellow plotters decamped to Hainault, a French-speaking principality of the Holy Roman Empire which was beyond her brother's jurisdiction. There, she made a deal with the count, William I. She agreed to marry her son, who was now nearly fourteen years old, to the count's daughter Philippa. In return, William agreed to provide her with 700 troops under the command of his younger brother John and ships to carry them to England. On 24 September 1326, the little fleet arrived off the Suffolk port of Orwell. Such was the hatred in England for Edward II and the Despensers that their government collapsed almost at once. Men flocked to the queen's banner. London rose in her support. The court fled to the West Country, pursued by Isabella and her growing pack. Prince Edward was proclaimed 'keeper' of the realm and all his father's powers were vested in him. The elder Despenser was caught at Bristol, the younger on the Welsh march. They were summarily condemned as traitors and put to death. All of these things were done in Prince Edward's name, but it is unlikely that he had any real say. We can only guess at his thoughts.

Edward II was imprisoned in Kenilworth Castle while Parliament met at Westminster to decide on his fate. On 13 January 1327, Parliament resolved to depose him. He was, they said, 'incompetent to govern in person'.[6] At Kenilworth, Edward II was brought into the great hall to face the parliamentary commissioners. There, groaning and weeping, he renounced the throne in favour of his eldest son. Shortly, the old king was moved to Berkeley Castle, where in due course he was discreetly murdered. On 1 February 1327, Edward III was crowned in Westminster Abbey. He was just fourteen years old. Real power was exercised by Mortimer and Isabella.

These events were profoundly shocking to contemporary sensibilities. The discarding of an anointed king, thinly disguised as an abdication; the flaunted adultery of the queen, publicly justified by putting it about that her husband wanted to kill her with his own hands; the blatant exercise of power and accumulation of lands and riches by Mortimer, a man of modest birth who held no office of state and technically was not even a member of the king's council. The government of Mortimer and Isabella was intensely hated. It proved to be just as vindictive, despotic and unstable as that of the Despensers but a great deal less competent. Because of its domestic weakness it was obliged to submit to fresh humiliations at the hands of both the Scots and the French.

The Scots, seeing chaos returning to England, returned to the old pattern of raids into the northern counties and Ireland. An English army marched north in the summer of 1327 to confront them in the Wear valley. The young king accompanied the army in his mother's baggage train, nominally in command of the campaign but in reality a mere cipher. The campaign was an expensive and public failure. The Scots avoided battle and vanished into thin air whenever the enemy approached. Edward wept tears of frustration and humiliation. Early the following year, England entered into a treaty with the Scots known as the Treaty of Northampton (after the town where it was ratified by Parliament). Its terms completed the king's humiliation. He was made to abandon all of the pretensions conceived three decades earlier by Edward I. Robert Bruce was recognized as King of Scotland and Edward's own claims renounced. At the same time, the Scots were expressly permitted to retain their alliance with the French. In England it became known as the 'shameful peace'. It was widely believed that Edward had protested but had been ignored.

In February 1328, Charles IV of France died, leaving only daughters. It had already been established that the throne of France could not be occupied by a woman. That left two candidates. The first was Edward III of England, whose mother was the last surviving child of Philip the Fair. He was the closest male relative of the dead king. The alternative was Philip of Valois, who was descended in unbroken male line from Philip III, the last King of France but four. Edward's claim never seems to have been given any serious consideration in France. Philip assumed the crown with the unanimous approval of the French nobility. The legal reason given at the time was that if Isabella had no right to the throne, she could not transmit one to her son. A century later, the propagandists of the dynasty invoked the so-called Salic Law of the Franks in support of this theory. But the real reason for Edward's exclusion was much simpler. Philip was the head of a considerable political connection in France, whereas Edward was a foreigner, an outsider and a potential enemy.

In May 1328, shortly before Philip VI's coronation, an English embassy arrived in Paris to protest at this turn of events. Their complaint was brushed aside and the ambassadors threatened with violence. When Philip, among his first acts, called on Edward to cross the Channel to do homage for Gascony, his ambassadors were told by Isabella that 'the son of a king would not do homage to the son of a count'. 'Typical of a woman,' says the chronicler who tells us this.[7] But it was not a sustainable line, and a few months later Mortimer and Isabella made peace with France. Edward was packed off to Amiens, where he performed a grudging (and in French eyes incomplete) public homage before an immense crowd in the cathedral. In England, where the political community had never attached much value to the French domains of the kings, these events aroused little interest. But Edward himself would remember them in later life as humiliating rebuffs, all the more mortifying for coming from his own cousins.

The past five years had given Edward an intensity of experience which was unusual even by the standards of an age which did not shelter children from injustice and cruelty. He was now, in 1329, technically of age, a married man and awaiting the birth of his first child. Yet he was excluded from power. His expenditure was tightly controlled. His acts were monitored. Spies were placed in his household to report on his doings. He was rarely allowed to travel save in his mother's company. Although few signs of protest were allowed to escape from the king's household, it is clear that Edward bitterly resented his artificial position. He sent his friend and mentor William Montagu to the papal court to warn the pope in confidence that the king was not his own master. His tutor and private secretary, Richard Bury, sent a specimen of his handwriting to Rome, with a secret code (the words *Pater sancte*) by which the papal court would know whether his letters represented his own wishes or had been dictated by Mortimer and Isabella. The king had already determined to free himself from his leading reins.

In the course of 1330, tensions rose at court. Mortimer's enemies began to spread rumours that Edward II was still alive. A plot was discovered to foment a rising in the old king's name. Edward II's half-brother the Earl of Kent, who was implicated, was summarily condemned to death. There were reports that Isabella was pregnant with Mortimer's child, and that the pair planned to usurp the throne. Montagu persuaded the young Edward that the time had come to act: 'Better to eat the dog, than let the dog eat you.'[8] In mid October 1330, there was a scene in the keep of Nottingham Castle, where the court was then staying. Edward's companions and attendants were summoned before the council. Mortimer told them that Edward was plotting against the government, and accused them of abetting him. It was an extraordinary thing to say about a man who was king and of full age. But Mortimer's fears were justified. A few days later, on the night of 19 October 1330, Edward III, Montagu and about a dozen companions suborned the captain of the castle and found their way into the inner bailey by an underground culvert, evading Mortimer's bodyguards. They burst into Isabella's apartment, where they found her preparing for bed. Mortimer was in an adjoining room with some friends. There was a fight. Two of Mortimer's attendants were killed and a third executed on the spot. Several others were wounded. 'Fair son, have pity on noble Mortimer,' Isabella is said to have cried.[9] Both of them were arrested.

A proclamation was issued, repudiating all that they had done in his name and announcing that Edward would from now on rule in person. Parliament was summoned. Mortimer was in due course sent to London, where he was condemned unheard and became the first person ever to be executed at Tyburn. As for Isabella, she was banished to her dower lands and remained out of public view for most of the rest of her life. She died twenty-eight years later at the age of sixty-six. Proprieties were observed to the end. She was buried in the robes that she had worn when, as a twelve-year-old girl, she had married the man whom she later connived in murdering.

2

The Challenge of War

(1330–1337)

When Edward III mounted the throne, the English enjoyed a poor reputation as warriors. 'In my youth,' wrote the Italian poet Petrarch, 'they were regarded as the most timid of the uncouth races . . . lower even than the miserable Scots.'[1] The chronicler Jean le Bel of Liège, who had taken part in the campaign of 1327 against the Scots, agreed. No one rated them or spoke of their courage or skill, he recalled, and their equipment looked distinctly old-fashioned beside the gleaming plate armour of continental armies.[2]

These contemporaries credited Edward III with a military revolution. In fact the revolution was already underway when he came to the throne. A number of important developments had come together to produce this result. In the first place, the English had learned earlier than any of their continental rivals the importance of military administration. Under the pressures of the Scottish and Welsh wars of the past half-century, they had developed a formidable bureaucratic machine not just for recruiting armies, but for requisitioning transport and shipping, collecting, storing and distributing supplies, maintaining field pay offices and for mass-producing equipment. Secondly, the English armed their bowmen with the six-foot longbow, a weapon peculiar to the British Isles which was to give them a decisive advantage on European battlefields. Volleys of iron-tipped arrows loosed in rapid succession high over the heads of the enemy proved to be devastatingly effective, penetrating chain mail and causing carnage in the tightly packed formations of infantry and cavalry. The standard equipment in use on the continent was the wooden cross-bow, a cumbersome weapon with a shorter range and a very slow rate of fire. By the end of Edward I's reign, the longbow had displaced the crossbow in English armies, and by the 1320s longbowmen were well on the way to displacing other infantrymen. Increasingly, they tended to be mounted, giving English armies a unique mobility.

Thirdly, at a time when the massed cavalry charge with couched lances was the main technique of knightly war-fare, the English had largely abandoned it, preferring to dismount their cavalry to fight on foot. They had learned this lesson from the Scots, who had fought off the cavalry charges of their enemies by drawing up their infantry in squares, planting their pikes in the ground pointing out-wards to the approaching horsemen. The shattering defeat of the English cavalry at Bannockburn (1314) had been an awful warning. It was, a contemporary wrote, 'unheard of in our time for such an army to be scattered by infantry, until we remember how the flower of France fell before the Flemings at Courtrai'.[3] The French would eventually learn this lesson, but the English learned it quicker.

These developments were symptomatic of a more fundamental change in English aristocratic society. Earlier generations had been instinctively hostile to military service except in Scotland and Wales whose subjugation could be regarded as essential to the security of England. Edward I and Edward II had both recruited their cavalry by means of feudal summonses, while infantry were conscripted in their counties by special commissioners of array. Even so, they had encountered serious recruitment problems and sometimes outright opposition. Edward III issued no feudal summons after 1327. Apart from a brief experiment in 1346 with conscription according to income, the cavalry who fought in his armies were all volunteers serving with their companies for pay, loot and honour. The same was increasingly true of the archers. Soldiers were recruited by captains who had contracted with the king (or some great lord) to raise a company for his service. They fought together with their friends, neighbours and dependants, sometimes year after year in the same retinues, contributing to the progressive militarization of English society.

As a soldier, Edward III was formed, like many of his captains, by the experience of fighting in Scotland. Although the king had bitterly resented the 'shameful' peace of Northampton, he did not originally set out to destroy it. He was an opportunist, not a plotter. The opportunity to intervene again in Scotland arose from an unexpected turn of events in the summer of 1332. In August, a small private army of English and French adventurers landed from the sea in Fife. The expedition had been organized by an

Anglo-French adventurer, Henry Beaumont, with the aid of a group of the 'disinherited'. These were men who had received offices and land in Scotland during the brief period of occupation by Edward I, from which they had been expelled by Robert Bruce in his time of triumph. The Treaty of Northampton provided for their restoration, a provision which the Scots had so far failed to observe. Their figurehead was Edward Balliol, the son of Edward I's puppet-king and perhaps the most 'disinherited' of all. Scotland was vulnerable in 1332. Robert Bruce was dead, and the country was governed by a regency in the name of his eight-year-old son, David II. The Guardian of Scotland, Donald Earl of Mar, raised an army to confront the invaders. It outnumbered them many times over. But five days after the landing it was wiped out at the Battle of Dupplin Moor. Most of the Scottish host never reached the enemy lines. They were massacred by archers as they tried to advance. Much of Lowland Scotland rallied to Balliol's cause. Six weeks after the battle, he was crowned King of Scotland at Scone, publicly proclaiming his allegiance to the crown of England and calling on Edward III to support him. In return, he declared himself ready to cede much of southern Scotland to the English king.

Edward III had known in advance of Balliol's adventure, and may even have secretly accepted his homage for the kingdom of Scotland. But the outcome took him by surprise. During the autumn of 1332, he tried to raise support and finance for an expedition to support Balliol against the inevitable Scottish counter-attack. But he was too late. Shortly before Christmas, the new Guardian of

Scotland, Archibald Douglas, caught Edward Balliol at night at Annan on the Solway Forth. Most of Balliol's companions were killed, and he himself fled through the night to England. The only way in which his cause could now be sustained was for Edward III to mount a full-scale invasion of Scotland and put Balliol on the throne by force.

In March 1333, two English armies entered Scotland, one by the west march under Edward Balliol and the other by the east march under the king himself. Both armies converged on Berwick-on-Tweed, the principal Scottish fortress of the border, and laid siege to it. Major sieges of this kind were usually designed to provoke a pitched battle when the defenders tried to mount a relief operation. This is what happened in 1333. On 19 July a Scottish relief army under the command of Archibald Douglas approached Berwick. Edward III drew up his army two miles from the town at Halidon Hill. The cavalry dismounted in the centre of the line with their horses held at the rear ready for the pursuit, the archers at the wings, slightly forward of them, where they could pour arrows into the flanks of the enemy as they advanced on the English centre. This disposition of his forces followed the one used by Henry Beaumont and Edward Balliol at Dupplin Moor the year before, and was probably suggested by those who had been present. It became the classic English battle plan. Its efficacy depended on the enemy attacking first. As at Dupplin Moor, that is what the Scots did. They advanced on foot and threw themselves against the English lines. They were routed. Once again it was the archers who claimed most of the casualties on the field. Several thousand more were killed in the pursuit which followed. Douglas and five Scottish earls were among the dead.

The Battle of Halidon Hill was Edward III's first taste of victory, a milestone in his development as a soldier and a ruler. It also made his reputation with public opinion. 'Men freely declared,' a contemporary wrote, 'that the Scottish wars had come to an end, for nothing remained of the Scottish nation.'[4] At first it looked as if this prediction might be true. Berwick opened its gates to the besiegers. Edward Balliol was reinstated as King of Scotland, and set up his capital at Perth, protected by English lances. In June 1334, he met Edward III in the Dominican house at Newcastle to perform his promises. He ceded eight counties to England, comprising the whole of southern Scotland south of the Firth of Forth and the Solway Firth, and did homage for the rest of his newly won kingdom. David II, the young King of Scotland, fled to the castle of Dumbarton on the Clyde. From there, he took ship for France, where he was installed with his diminutive court in the fortress of Château-Gaillard in Normandy.

This dramatic turn in Scotland's fortunes produced an immediate crisis in Edward III's dealings with France. Relations between the two countries were already tense. The French king, Philip VI, was a man of imperious ways who was determined to press his government's rights in Aquitaine to the limit. Shortly after Edward had taken power in England, a new accommodation had been reached with Philip. Edward had agreed to treat the homage he had done at Amiens as liege homage, the strongest bond of allegiance known to feudal law. For their part, the

French agreed to set up a joint commission to restore at least some of the lands in Aquitaine which their armies had overrun since 1324. Edward was very secretive about these arrangements and clearly sensitive to the loss of face involved. He crossed the Channel in disguise with a handful of attendants and performed the act of homage privately at a royal hunting lodge north of Paris.

England's new accommodation with France was rapidly undermined by the revival of the Scottish war. The 'auld alliance', which had recently been renewed, bound the French to intervene if Scotland was attacked. Philip VI took this obligation seriously. He had already funded an attempt to bring supplies into Berwick during the siege, and he contributed to the expenses of David II's exiled court in France. He sent weapons and other supplies by sea to the enclaves of western Scotland still held by David's supporters. Worse, he refused to consider restoring the provinces of Aquitaine which had been occupied in the 1320s, unless Edward came to terms with David II. A succession of embassies crossed the Channel in the hope of negotiating a settlement. They were met with a succession of obdurate rebuffs. This was a critical development. English public opinion had always regarded the subjugation of Scotland as a higher priority than the defence of Aquitaine. By linking the two issues in this way, Philip VI provoked a radical change in English attitudes to the prospect of war with France.

In the summer of 1334, there was a major rebellion against the regime of Edward Balliol in Scotland. For the second time, Balliol's cause collapsed and he himself was obliged to flee. As a result, Edward led his army once more into Scotland in November of that year. This time, the Scots were determined to revert to Robert Bruce's old strategy and avoid a pitched battle. For the English, the campaign was a disaster. The worst winter in living memory made movement extremely difficult for the invaders. After three months laying waste to much of the western lowlands, Edward III ran out of money and withdrew to England. Arriving back at Newcastle in February 1335, he found a French embassy waiting for him with an angry protest against the invasion and a proposal to mediate between the English king and the leaders of the Scots. Edward agreed to this. But it soon became clear that he had no intention of making peace with the Scots on any terms but his own. He was already planning a fresh invasion of Scotland in the summer.

In the second week of July 1335, the English entered Scotland again. They invaded in two columns under Edward's command. Once again, his troops burned everything before them. Once again, the Scots avoided battle. Once again, Edward was left beating the air. Meanwhile, in Paris the French government announced its intention of restoring David II by force to his throne. A seaborne expeditionary force of 6,000 soldiers was planned, which would sail for Scotland as soon as the men and ships could be found. For a time, nothing happened, but in the summer of 1336, it began to look as if the French were serious. The size of the proposed expeditionary force was increased. A fleet of 200 transports, escorted by 60 supply ships and 30 war galleys, was planned. It would have been the largest amphibious operation in Europe since the army of the Fifth Crusade had landed in Egypt a century before. The landing area was to be on the east coast of Scotland between the Moray Firth and the Firth of Tay. Two of David II's companions in France were sent to organize support in Scotland. A small advance guard of French knights arrived in Aberdeen to prepare for the coming of the French army. A secondary force was planned which would land in southern England in the hope of pinning down English forces there.

The French never launched their invasion. Philip VI's advisers had underestimated the cost and the logistical problems involved. And the expedition was finally made almost impossible by a bold stroke on the part of Edward III. He was receiving detailed information about French plans and preparations from well-placed spies in Paris and the North Sea ports. In June 1336, he entered Scotland with a handful of men and arrived without warning at Stirling. From here he advanced to Perth. Both of these places had English garrisons. At Perth, he succeeded in collecting a small army from garrison troops and reinforcements brought to him from England. With these, he marched north to the Moray Firth and then made his way down the coast, engaging in an orgy of destruction. All the animals that could be found were rounded up and slaughtered. The ripening crops were burned in the fields. The food stores were emptied. Aberdeen's churches were spared, but the town was reduced to a mass of charred stumps. Without the port facilities of the region or local supplies of food, the French invasion had become impractical.

While Edward was in Scotland, an English embassy was in Paris trying to ward off the threat of war. On 20 August they appeared before Philip VI to receive his final answer. It was bleak. Philip told them that he was determined to invade both England and Scotland in support of David II. His preparations, he said, were well underway. According to reports circulating in England, the French king said that there would never be peace until the same king ruled in France, England and Scotland. At the end of September 1336, a great council gathered at Nottingham to consider the ambassadors' sombre reports from France. It comprised the king's permanent council, the parliamentary peerage and representatives of the shires and boroughs. Edward himself hurried south from Scotland to join them. He found his councillors in the grip of war fever. Armed French ships had already begun to raid along the south and east coasts, seizing English and Gascon merchantmen. English ships had been captured at Orwell and in the Solent. Beacons were being built along the coasts to warn of the appearance of an invasion fleet. The county levies were called out, a total of 80,000 men, to defend the coasts. Merchant ships were being requisitioned for war service. Rumours flew about of saboteurs and fifth columnists. French merchants in England were arrested and thrown in prison. In France, the government retaliated in kind.

At some time during the autumn of 1336, the French cancelled their projected invasion. The logistical challenges finally proved to be too great. But politically, they had passed the point of no return. Frustrated in his projects against England, Philip VI turned his attention to

Aquitaine, which was a great deal more vulnerable. For his part, Edward III virtually abandoned his attempt to subjugate Scotland and shifted his priorities to meet the new threat from across the Channel. His capital, which had been temporarily installed at York for the past four years, was transferred back to Westminster, closer to the chief peril facing the realm, as he explained to Parliament. Balliol, whose lack of support in Scotland was palpable, had by now withdrawn permanently to England. The English were progressively being driven out of their enclaves north of the Forth. Over the following years they focused all their efforts on trying to hang on to the regions south of the Forth which Balliol had ceded to them. Edward almost certainly expected to return to Scotland once he had dealt with the threat from France. But as the king's continental ambitions claimed ever more of his attention and resources, this came to seem unrealistic. The war with France eventually cost Edward all of his Scottish conquests and saved Scottish independence. As a Scottish chronicler sang:

> It wes to Scotland a gud chance
> That thai made thaim to werrey in France[5]

By the end of 1336, it was clear that Philip VI was looking for an excuse to confiscate the duchy of Aquitaine. Edward had given him plenty of legal grounds. His officials were involved in a large number of lawsuits in the Parlement, and in some of them he was in contempt of its orders. French officials who arrived in the duchy to execute a judgment for damages were sent away with oaths ringing in their ears. But the ground eventually chosen for forfeiting the duchy was a different one. Edward III was sheltering in England a fugitive from French justice, Philip VI's brother-in-law Robert of Artois, who had been accused of forging documents to prove a claim to the county of Artois. Robert was a violent and dishonest adventurer with many enemies. But he was also flamboyant and charming, an excellent horseman and a skilful flatterer, in fact just the kind of man that Edward liked. Although Robert was in England, where Edward was the sovereign, Philip chose to treat this as a breach of his obligations as Duke of Aquitaine. In December 1336, Philip sent a notice to the English seneschal of Gascony demanding Robert's extradition, and announcing that the Master of the Royal Archers, Étienne le Galois de la Baume, would follow with orders to enforce the demand. Etienne arrived on the Gascon march in February and tried to seize the English border town of Saint-Macaire. When the gates were closed against him, he tried to call up artillery to force an entrance. At Westminster, Parliament met in March 1337. It authorized the delivery of an ultimatum to Philip VI and granted a tax to fund the despatch of an army to France. No fewer than six new peers were created, including several of the companions who had helped the king to seize power from Mortimer and Isabella in 1330. No one suggested that there was any further scope for diplomacy.

In May 1337, the King of France summoned a great council to Paris to consider the next step. On their authority, he resolved to confiscate Aquitaine. The English seneschal in the duchy was a Norfolk knight, Sir Oliver Ingham, an able and experienced administrator but with no money and few men at his disposal. Two French royal officers appeared before him at Libourne with the documents pronouncing the decree of confiscation. They demanded that all ducal towns and castles should be surrendered to them at once. Ingham tried in vain to negotiate a delay to enable him to obtain instructions. The officers told him that an army of occupation was already on its way. This was true. At the beginning of July, the Constable of France, Raoul, Count of Eu, marched down the Garonne with a large French army at his back. His plan was to march on Bordeaux.

Ingham adopted the only course open to him. He and his captains abandoned the open country to the enemy and shut themselves behind the walls of their strongholds by the coast, hoping that the danger would pass. To their own surprise and relief, it did. The Count of Eu was a very mediocre commander and his campaign had been poorly prepared. In September 1337, after failing before Bordeaux and capturing some minor towns and castles, he was recalled to the north and his army disbanded. Edward III had contributed nothing to the salvation of the duchy. His eyes were fixed on northern France.

3
'King of France'
(1337–1347)

The shift of attention from Scotland to France brought
Edward III face to face with strategic and logistical problems which would confront the English for the rest of the
century. The only parts of Aquitaine which were capable
of defending themselves were the cities of Bordeaux and
Bayonne. They were both rich cities with stout walls, large
populations and enough money to hire professional troops
to man them. The rest of the duchy was defenceless without significant reinforcements from England. Getting an
English army to south-western France raised serious logistical problems. To get there by sea called for very large
numbers of merchant ships. At this stage, the English merchant marine was probably larger than it had ever been, or
would ever be again until the sixteenth century. It comprised at least 700 seagoing vessels. But only the largest of
these vessels were suitable for the long passage round the
Breton cape and across the Bay of Biscay. Even those had
limited deck space. They could rarely carry more than ten
fully equipped soldiers with their attendants and horses
and fodder and water for the journey. The alternative was
to land them on a hostile coast in northern France and

march them overland to Bordeaux. But the great west-flowing rivers, the Seine and the Loire, were formidable barriers to any army moving from north to south. Avoiding them would involve passing far to the east through the Massif Central, a march of some 800 miles, which was only once attempted in the whole of the fourteenth century, and then with disastrous results.

This meant that to defend Aquitaine it was necessary to attack in the north in the hope of pressuring the French government into making concessions. The main instrument of English warfare in France would be the *chevauchée*, a powerful long-distance mounted raid, accompanied by the deliberate destruction of the country. It was a form of terrorism. The object was to force the French government's hand by fear: fear of fire, rapine and looting; fear of large-scale regional defections by men worried about losing their land; and fear of having the king's inability to defend his realm exposed, unless he took the risk of engaging the enemy in battle. The strategy rarely worked. But it was all that the English could do, short of setting up a permanent military occupation of parts of France. They did from time to time try to do this, generally with the aid of local opponents of the Valois dynasty and money extracted from the local populations. But a permanent military occupation proved to be beyond England's resources, and there was rarely enough local support to make any difference to the French government's calculations.

The king's natural allies in this venture were to be found in Germany. It was an approach which had been tried by King John and Edward I in their time, and would remain a central theme of English strategic thinking until the age of Chatham and Pitt the Younger. Fourteenth-century Germany was a loose confederation of princely states which extended well beyond the limits of modern-day Germany to include what is now the Netherlands, eastern Belgium, the francophone provinces east of the Saône and the Rhone and much of northern Italy. Its nominal ruler, known as the 'King of the Romans', was Louis of Bavaria, a German prince nominated by an electoral college but possessing no power of command and no resources other than those that he could find from his own hereditary lands.

The task of building Edward III's coalition fell to a roving English embassy led by Henry Burghersh, Bishop of Lincoln, who was currently Edward's chief foreign policy adviser, and the king's confidant William Montagu, recently promoted to the peerage as Earl of Salisbury. They embarked on a tour of western Germany recruiting allies who were willing to support the English in an invasion of northern France. By the time Burghersh and Montagu returned to England, in August 1337, they had obtained commitments amounting to nearly 7,000 troops. Louis declared his intention of leading the German contingents in person. But in case he was unable to do this, he promised to appoint Edward as his Vicar General to conduct the war on his behalf. Louis had his own disputes with France, whose gradual expansion into the territories of the empire in the Rhineland and the Low Countries had provoked fear and resentment among the princes of the region.

But the real reason why the Germans signed up to the coalition was that they were bribed. Edward's ambassadors had promised a total of over £120,000 a year in annuities. Thousands more were paid out in gifts to their councillors. In addition to the annuities and bribes, Edward would have to pay the wages of the German companies when the campaign opened. The total cost of the army, including the 10,000 English troops which he expected to bring to the continent himself, was likely to exceed £200,000. The whole bill would come to several times the English king's income, even after taking into account the generous taxes voted by Parliament in March 1337.

Finance was always Edward III's weak point. He had little understanding of the problems of taxation or credit and was bored by administration. He tended to fund his enterprises on a hand-to-mouth basis, without budgets or forecasts. To fill the gap in 1337, he turned to a consortium of financiers organized by England's most famous merchant, William Pole of Hull. Pole and his associates devised a high-risk scheme to fund the campaign by rigging the English wool market. Raw wool was England's chief export and it was indispensable for the textile manufacturers of Flanders and the Low Countries. The idea was that the government would compulsorily purchase the year's entire wool crop on credit. The consortium proposed to ship the wool to the Low Countries, where it would be sold at inflated monopoly prices. After the producers had received their price and the financiers their profit, the surplus was expected to produce the £200,000 required by the king in two instalments, in December 1337 and May 1338.

Everything went wrong. The original plan was that the army would sail for Antwerp towards the end of 1337. This was never realistic and the expedition had to be postponed to the following year. Meanwhile, it took longer than expected to buy and ship the wool and only about a third of it had reached the continent by the end of 1337. The delays rattled the German princes, and forced Bishop Burghersh to negotiate a postponement of the payment of their annuities and advances. But Pole's consortium was unable to produce the money even by the revised date. In the end, Burghersh seized the wool which had reached Holland and sold it at the best price he could get, thereby flooding the market, destroying the consortium and raising only about a sixth of the money required to pay the German princes. When the king finally arrived at Antwerp, in July 1338, he brought with him a modest army of just 4,400 men, less than half the number originally planned. There was no wool, no money and no German army. By borrowing on usurious terms in England and Italy, Edward was eventually able to raise enough to pay Louis of Bavaria and some of the princes. Edward and Louis met at a splendid ceremony at Coblenz on the Rhine in September 1338, at which Edward was solemnly invested as Vicar General of the Holy Roman Empire. But it was already clear that the invasion would have to be postponed again. The opening of the campaign was refixed for May 1339. The king returned to Antwerp, where he and his court passed the winter in idleness, eating up supplies and money and keeping the enterprise going with worthless promises and ruinous borrowing. Back in England, the coasts were relentlessly attacked by French warships. Southampton was sacked. Morale collapsed.

The winter and spring were passed in a desperate attempt to raise funds in time for the start of the campaign. Edward's attempt to manipulate the wool trade had failed. Driven back upon his English revenues, he gradually lost touch with reality. He borrowed improvidently. Fresh subsidies were squeezed out of Parliament. Edward bombarded his ministers in England with orders, rebukes and complaints. He attributed the lack of funds reaching him in Antwerp to mismanagement and treachery, when it was actually due to the attempt to finance war simultaneously in Gascony, the Low Countries and the march of Scotland on a scale well beyond the resources of his realm, in addition to carrying on the ordinary functions of government. He would have stopped the salaries of the ministers and officials if he had not been warned that they would resign en masse.

In the event, it was not until September 1339 that Edward III finally launched his campaign, four months late, from Valenciennes in Hainault. But he was unable to bring the French to battle. Philip VI knew that Edward could not afford a long campaign. So he refused to offer his enemy the decisive battle which he needed, simply waiting for him to run out of money. After burning villages and crops across a wide front, in the hope that this would shame the French king into fighting him, Edward finally confronted the French army on 23 October 1339 outside the village of La Capelle, east of Cambrai. Each side drew up its strength in battle order, and waited for the other to abandon the protection of its trenches and fieldworks and attack. Neither of them moved. Towards the end of the afternoon, Philip VI sounded the retreat. The English taunted their enemies with cowardice. But Edward knew that Philip's departure spelled the failure of his campaign.

The year 1340 saw a new beginning, this time in alliance with another of France's hostile neighbours on the north, the county of Flanders. Flanders was nominally a province of France. But it had for many years been practically independent under the counts of the house of Dampierre. The county was the most heavily industrialized region of northern Europe, and its important cloth industry was heavily dependent on English wool. This placed it in an ambiguous position between England and France. In December 1337 and January 1338, there was a revolution in the industrial towns of Flanders, led by an unscrupulous demagogue from Ghent, Jacob van Artevelde. His policy was summed up in the words attributed to him by a French chronicler: 'Flanders lives by making cloth, and cloth cannot be made without wool. It follows that we must make a friend of England.'[1] As fears grew of French intervention in support of the count, the new regime drew closer to England. By the end of 1339 they were ready to enter into a defensive and offensive alliance with Edward III.

Up to this point, Edward had not publicly claimed the throne of France. He had a passable claim, which he had almost certainly waived by doing homage (twice) to the French king, Philip VI. The possibility of reviving it had been considered several times at Westminster, and was discussed in Parliament in March 1337. It seems to have been quietly dropped, possibly on the advice of the Lords. It was Van Artevelde and his friends who finally persuaded

Edward to put it forward again. Their motives were straightforward. They wanted to legitimize their assumption of power. They wanted to recover the old districts of Walloon Flanders around Lille and Douai, which had been annexed by France forty years before after the previous rising of the Flemish towns. And they wanted other political benefits such as a reformed coinage. Only if he claimed to be King of France could Edward III confer these things on the Flemings. From his point of view the claim was a useful tool of propaganda. It made it easier for the English king to find allies among powerful malcontents in Philip's realm who needed some legal cover for rebellion. It also greatly simplified Edward's diplomatic position on Aquitaine. If he was King of France, then at least in theory the feudal status of Aquitaine no longer mattered. So, on 26 January 1340, Edward III arrived at Ghent, then the largest town of Flanders and the leading power behind the revolution. Standing with his allies and friends on a platform in the Friday Market decked out with banners of the arms of England crossed with those of France, he was proclaimed King of France by a crowd of cheering Flemings.

Edward's decision to declare himself King of France was perhaps his most famous political act, and arguably his most enduring legacy (his successors used the title until 1802). The claim to the French throne is commonly supposed to have been the origin of the Hundred Years War. In fact the claim had very little to do with the causes of the war, and Edward did not proclaim himself King of France until some time after the conflict had begun. It was a

classic piece of Edwardian opportunism. It was never realistic, except perhaps for a brief decade in the 1420s, and
was never taken seriously by more than a handful of people in France. It is difficult to know how seriously it was
taken by Edward himself. It is clear from his stance in successive diplomatic conferences that he regarded it as a
bargaining counter. He was always ready to trade it for
territory. His problem was that he could never openly
acknowledge this without loss of face. As one of Edward's
ambassadors pointed out a few years later, dropping the
claim would be tantamount to admitting that he had set
out to conquer a kingdom that was not his, and launched
himself upon an unjust war. So the claim survived to
poison successive diplomatic conferences and mock the
failures of Edward's later years.

In February 1340, Edward managed to extricate himself
from the clutch of his creditors and return briefly to England to raise money and reinforcements, leaving his wife
and son and two earls behind as hostages in Flanders for
his return. The attention of both sides now switched to the
North Sea. Philip VI, determined to stop him returning to
the continent, raised a fleet of more than 200 ships. His
'Great Army of the Sea' consisted mainly of sailing ships
requisitioned from merchants. But there were also nearly
thirty oared barges and galleys, the nearest that the fourteenth century came to specialized warships. For his part,
Edward had collected a fleet of merchantmen about
150 strong to fight his way past the French fleet. These had
been requisitioned in English ports, built up with timber
'castles' fore and aft, and filled with pressed crews and

soldiers. Early in June, the French fleet arrived in the estuary north of the port of Sluys in northern Flanders, and waited for Edward to appear. In England, Edward's ministers advised him to drop the invasion. It was too risky now, they said. They were supported by the professional seamen in charge of the shipping arrangements. Edward, in a vile temper, accused them of plotting against him. He ordered the ships to collect at Orwell and the army to embark.

On Midsummer's Day, 24 June 1340, early in the afternoon, the English fleet entered the great enclosed bay of Sluys. The French fleet was arrayed before them in three lines of anchored ships, like an army on land. The ships of the first line were chained together to make an impassable barrier. The English bore down on them and collided with the leading enemy vessels. After four hours of fierce fighting from the decks, with bows and arrows and boarding parties, the English had destroyed the front line. The rest of the enemy tried to escape in the failing evening light. Few of them succeeded. By nightfall, the English had destroyed or captured all but 23 of the 213 French ships. Between 16,000 and 18,000 French seamen and soldiers had lost their lives, including all of Philip VI's admirals. Edward himself had been in the thick of the fighting and had been wounded by an arrow in the thigh.

It was a remarkable victory. But it was to be the prelude to months of frustration and disappointment. Edward had a very small army with him in Flanders. There may have been as few as 2,000 men. For his fighting strength, he depended mainly on mobs of poorly trained and ill-disciplined soldiers recruited in the towns of Flanders, and some companies of professional troops supplied by his remaining German allies. Edward ran out of money to pay these men before the campaign even started. He borrowed heavily from Flemish merchants and Florentine banking houses. At one point three English earls who had stood as guarantors of the king's debts to local moneylenders were arrested and locked in a debtors' prison at Mechelen in Brabant. Eventually, at the end of July, Edward marched on Tournai with his creditors yapping at his heels. Tournai was an autonomous city-state on the River Scheldt on the eastern border of Flanders, which belonged to its bishop but was under French protection. Edward had had to undertake the siege of this place to satisfy his Flemish allies. But unless it drew the French to battle, it served no strategic purpose of his own. Philip VI had no intention of being drawn to battle. So Edward sat outside the walls for two months, while his army, weakened by disease, desertions and casualties, gradually wasted away.

On 25 September 1340, the king, unable to pay his remaining troops, agreed to a truce. Edward had been defeated by weaknesses of conception and entirely foreseeable failures of execution. His three-year obsession with the Low Countries and Germany had cost him terrible losses in other theatres of war. In Aquitaine, his officers had lost about a third of the duchy's surviving territory, while in Scotland they had lost most of the land south of the Forth and the Clyde which he had overrun during the 1330s. The following year, the Scottish cause would be sufficiently secure to allow David II to return from his exile in France. Edward returned to Ghent after the campaign, a prisoner of his creditors. At the end of November, he was obliged to steal surreptitiously away from the city at dawn and take ship for England, leaving most of his companions behind.

The king returned to a bankrupt treasury and a major political crisis. The latest parliamentary subsidies had brought in much less than expected. Another attempt to seize the wool crop had failed. The mood in England had become increasingly ugly, as an exhausted nation sullenly resisted Edward's collectors. The king understood none of this. As always, he put his failure down to the incompetence and corruption of his ministers in England, who in his hour of need had failed to send him money that was not there to be sent. Arriving by boat in the middle of the night at the water gate of the Tower of London, he summoned them from their beds, to be summarily dismissed and in some cases imprisoned. The chief of them, Archbishop Stratford of Canterbury, fled to sanctuary in his cathedral. From there he launched a sustained propaganda war against the king, accusing him of tyranny and financial extortion, and comparing him with his father. The rift threatened to summon up all the old ghosts of the previous reign which Edward thought had been laid to rest. But Edward was not like his father. He was prepared to make concessions to his enemies. He still enjoyed the support of the higher nobility. These advantages enabled him to survive the crisis.

Misfortune did nothing to dent his determination. 'My power has not been laid so low and the hand of God is not yet so weak that I cannot with his grace prevail over my enemy,' he wrote to the Doge of Genoa.[2] Within a year, a fresh opportunity presented itself to intervene in France with the aid of continental allies, this time in Brittany. Like Flanders, Brittany was a virtually autonomous province of France, governed by its own dukes. In April 1341, the Duke of Brittany died without leaving a direct male heir. The succession was contested between the dead man's half-brother, John de Montfort, and Charles of Blois, one of the greatest territorial magnates of the province. Charles also had the support of the French king and of most of the baronage of Brittany, and the backing of the Parlement of Paris, which ruled that he had the better claim in law. At the end of 1341, John was overwhelmed and taken off to Paris as a prisoner. In his absence, his wife appealed to the English for help.

Brittany was of great strategic importance to the English kings. It stood across the sea route to Gascony as well as providing the most convenient overland route. Edward responded to the countess's appeal with alacrity but with very little regard for either the logistical problems or the limits of his resources. It took him several months to raise a modest army, and even longer to requisition a fleet. The first troops reached the duchy in April 1342. But Edward himself did not arrive with the main body of the army until October. His main object was to capture the two major maritime cities of southern Brittany, Vannes and Nantes. Vannes would have given him a sheltered port on the south side of the peninsula, and Nantes a secure crossing of the Loire. But he failed before both places. His problem in Brittany was the same as it had been on the northern frontier in 1339 and 1340. Philip VI played a waiting game, refusing battle and waiting for the English to run out of money. In January 1343, after just three months in the field, Edward agreed to another truce in the town of Malestroit.

It was a poor return for so much effort. But the effort was not completely wasted, as the English retained a powerful presence in Brittany. A number of fortresses remained in their hands, including the important port of Brest. English companies continued the fight in the name of John de Montfort, conducting a persistent war of siege and ambush against the house of Blois. They sustained themselves by loot and by protection money extracted from the country around. It was a pattern which would eventually spread to all parts of France. Persisting until the end of the Hundred Years War, it would bring untold destruction and suffering to the French countryside, in the process making fortunes for some of Edward's captains but contributing little to English war aims.

Edward had to wait three years for his fortunes to turn. In June 1344, the English parliament was persuaded to finance what they hoped would be the final push that would force the French to terms. The grant, which extended over two years, was conditional on the king leading his army against the enemy in person. The king's strategy took shape gradually over the following months. In March 1345, John de Montfort, released from his French prison, fled to England, where he formally acknowledged Edward III as King of France and did homage to him for the duchy of Brittany.

Shortly after this, another political refugee arrived at

Edward's court, Godfrey of Harcourt, Lord of Saint-Sauveur-le-Vicomte in southern Normandy. Godfrey had led a rebellion against Philip VI in Normandy, and when it was snuffed out had fled the realm, first to Brabant and then to England. He was another volatile adventurer, a man of hopeless dreams rather like Robert of Artois. These exiles claimed great influence and large followings in France which they were willing to place at the English king's disposal. Naively, Edward believed them. With their assistance, an ambitious three-pronged attack was planned. An army would sail for Bordeaux under the command of Edward's cousin Henry of Grosmont, Earl of Derby. Another would make for Brittany under the joint command of the Earl of Northampton and John de Montfort. Both of these forces were expected to be swollen by the recruitment of local allies after they had landed. But the major operation would be a descent on the north, probably in Normandy, under Edward himself. These plans were conceived on an ambitious scale. The total deployment envisaged exceeded 20,000 men.

They proved to be too ambitious. In the event, the only notable military operations in 1345 were those of Henry of Grosmont in the south-west. He was the highest-ranking English nobleman and the best soldier to serve in Gascony for several decades. He defeated French armies in two battles in the course of the year and considerably expanded the area under effective English control. But the other ventures of that year were failures. Operations in Brittany came to a premature end when John de Montfort died of disease shortly after his arrival there. As for Edward's army, the fleet was on the point of sailing for France when news reached England of the imminent fall of Jacob van Artevelde's regime in Flanders. Flanders was no longer central to Edward's continental strategy, but it was the only province of France, apart from parts of Brittany and the south-west, where his claim to the French throne was recognized. Edward therefore felt bound to come to his old ally's assistance. He was unable to save Van Artevelde, who was lynched in the streets of Ghent while Edward's fleet lay off the coast at Sluys. By the time that the king returned to England, it was too late to rebuild momentum and invade France.

As it happened, the delay was providential, even if the habitually impatient king did not realize it. It enabled him to concentrate his resources and plan his operations more carefully for the following year. Edward was learning from his past failures. He was no longer willing to depend on expensive and fickle allies over whom he had no direct control. He now intended to fight using his own subjects, English and Gascon. When eventually Edward sailed for Normandy at the end of June 1346, his army numbered some 14,000 men, mostly mounted. It was the largest expeditionary force to sail for France in the whole of the Hundred Years War. There was also a primitive artillery train, a novelty in English warfare. About 750 ships manned by more than 15,000 seamen were deployed to carry this host, together with its horses and equipment, over the Channel.

Some of the troops had been conscripted, the last occasion when compulsion played a significant part in the recruitment of Edward's armies. But most of them were volunteers serving for adventure, honour and money. This remarkable reversal of the English nobility's traditional objection to foreign military service was arguably Edward III's most significant achievement. What lay behind it? At this stage of the war, it is unlikely that loot played much part. There had been precious little of that. A sense of status and social obligation counted for more. But the decisive factor was Edward himself. He involved the English nobility in his projects in a way that neither his father nor his grandfather had done. He treated them as friends and partners. He consulted them in Parliament and great councils. He listened to what they had to say, and they responded by giving him the advice that he wanted to hear.

Politically, Edward was adept at healing old wounds. Except in the case of Mortimer, he had avoided taking revenge on those responsible for the civil wars of the past two decades, and was generous with pardons for their supporters. 'We consider,' he declared when he created six new earls in 1337, 'that it is the chief mark of royalty that by the proper distribution of rank, honour and office, it buttresses itself with wise counsel and powerful men.'[3] As a result, Edward was the first King of England for two centuries to enjoy the unconditional political support of his most powerful subjects throughout his reign, until age and debility finally compelled him to withdraw from an active role in affairs.

Edward's chief asset was his personality. He was uncomplicated and likeable. He was flamboyant, extrovert and generous. His household and his war retinue became famous centres of chivalry. He presided at splendid entertainments at court. He was addicted to practical jokes and fancy-dress parties. He fought in the lists himself, with the same reckless courage that he would later show in battle. For his humbler subjects, it was enough that he behaved as a king was expected to behave, and favoured the sort of people whom a king was expected to favour. It is clear that even in their eyes he was more than a graven image of royalty. On campaign, he was capable of showing a common touch: pulling a bow at the butts with humble archers and playing the fool with his minstrels' kettle-drums. His household accounts have plenty of references to tips paid to ordinary people in whose houses he had rested on his travels, or small acts of generosity towards obscure individuals. The English army landed on the great open beach south of La Hougue in the Cotentin peninsula, a place that would become famous seven centuries later as Utah Beach. On a hill above the beach, the king knighted his sixteen-year-old son, Edward, Prince of Wales (the future 'Black Prince'), together with William Montagu, the son of the man who had organized his coup d'état in 1330, and Roger Mortimer, the son of its chief casualty. It was a symbolic moment.

The king's original plan was to set up a permanent occu-pation of southern Normandy, just as his officers had done in parts of western Brittany. Once he had done that, he planned to march up the Seine valley towards Paris in the hope that the threat to his capital would draw Philip VI into the decisive battle. The French were wrong-footed. They had expected him to land in the south-west. They had sent a large army to the march of Aquitaine under the command of Philip's eldest son, John, Duke of Normandy. He was currently engaged in besieging the fortress-town of Aiguillon at the confluence of the Lot and the Garonne. To meet the new threat, the French constable was obliged to improvise an army at short notice in the north. With this he hoped to hold the invaders behind the line of the River Orne. He decided to make a stand at Caen, the chief city of the Orne valley. But the defenders of Caen had not yet completed their arrangements when the English fell on them, and took the place by assault. The inhabitants were massacred and the army enriched with the spoil of the town. But Edward's victory was incomplete. The citadel of Caen still held out. With a major garrisoned fortress at his rear, the English king was obliged to abandon his plan to hold the Cotentin peninsula as a base for his return. Once he had challenged Philip outside Paris, he planned to make his line of retreat through northern France. His ministers in England were ordered to fit out a new fleet, which was to meet the army at Le Crotoy, a small port at the mouth of the Somme a few miles from Abbeville.

Edward's march on Paris encountered no serious resistance. The French stuck to the strategy of avoiding battle which they had followed for the past eight years and retreated before him. As they retreated, they broke the bridges over the Seine so as to keep him trapped south of the river. The English invaders penetrated as far as Poissy, just twelve miles from Paris. There, Edward decided to bolt for home. His engineers succeeded in building an improvised bridge over the Seine. After crossing on to the north side, the English army made for the Somme.

Edward III's abandonment of Normandy and his flight to the north were an admission that his strategy had failed. But his continued presence in France was viewed with dismay in Paris. The Parisians saw their country estates wasted by the invader. The nobility were being abused and mocked as cowards. Philip VI had not been defeated. But he had been humiliated, compelled to stand aside while an English army looted and burned its way with impunity across one of the richest provinces of France. Under the pressure of public opinion, Philip was finally forced to abandon the strategy of avoiding battle. He concentrated his forces in Paris and on the Somme. He ordered the Duke of Normandy to withdraw from Aiguillon and bring his army urgently north. Then he set out in pursuit of the enemy.

Edward had originally hoped to embark at the mouth of the Somme and escape across the Channel to England. But the fleet and the reinforcements and stores that he had expected to be waiting for him at Le Crotoy had not yet arrived. As a result, he decided to head north with a view to capturing a port or perhaps escaping into Flanders. For his part, Philip VI hoped to corner the English army against the Somme. His advance units reached the river ahead of Edward III and took possession of all the crossings. But the English king managed to reach the ford of Blanchetaque in the estuary of the river, and fought his way across it. Philip moved to cut the road further north. Edward halted outside the village of Crécy. There, the French army caught up on 26 August 1346. They were between 20,000 and 25,000 strong, including a large force of cavalry and several thousand Genoese crossbowmen. The English were waiting for them as they came up the road from Abbeville. Their cavalry and pikemen were drawn up in prepared positions, on rising ground with their backs to the forest, protected by a line of trenches and traps. The archers, about a third of the army, were posted at the wings, behind a defensive circle of baggage wagons. It was the tactical system that the English had perfected in Scotland. The French outnumbered them by nearly two to one. But the English had the advantage of the defensive and of better leadership. Philip was an unskilful tactician, and his captains were impetuous and overconfident.

At about five o'clock in the afternoon, the French attacked. They sent the Genoese crossbowmen forward first. But their crossbows were outranged by the longbows of the English, which inflicted carnage among them before they were able to shoot back. They fell back under the onslaught, and finally broke and fled. It was the first time that the French cavalry had witnessed the effects of massed longbowmen. They could not understand what was happening to the Genoese, and put their flight down to treachery. Without waiting for orders, the horsemen charged in impetuous disorder across the space between the two armies, trampling the Genoese underfoot. They headed for the centre of the English lines where the Prince of Wales was standing at the head of his division. As they came within range they encountered dense volleys of arrows. Their horses shied away and turned. Men began to fall wounded from their saddles. Those who succeeded in reaching the English lines were fought off in fierce hand-to-hand fighting.

The French rallied and charged many times. The Black Prince was in the thick of the fighting. Edward, directing the battle from a windmill at the crest of the hill, was urged to send in his reserve. 'Send no more to me for any adventure that may befall him as long as he is alive,' he is supposed to have answered, 'and say to them that sent you that they shall suffer him to win his spurs, for by God's will I will that this day be his.'[4] By the time that Edward finally committed his reserve, most of the French army was in full flight. In a last desperate attempt to restore the fortunes of battle, Philip VI's ally the blind King of Bohemia led his contingent into the thick of the battle. He was cut down along with nearly all his men. More than 1,500 French noblemen lay dead on the battlefield, in addition to hundreds more who were cut down in the pursuit. Their bodies were strewn across the fields for miles around. The French archers and infantry were massacred in thousands.

The French expected Edward III to return to England after his great victory. In fact, he did not. His finances had enjoyed a remarkable recovery. This was due partly to his selective repudiation of the debts accumulated during his earlier campaigns, and partly to generous new parliamentary subsidies. But the main factors were the buoyant state of the wool trade and the English customs revenues which depended on it, together with the skilful financial stewardship of William Edington, Bishop of Winchester, who had been appointed Treasurer of England in 1344. Edward was able to contemplate keeping his army in being through the winter. A few days after the Battle of Crécy, he and his captains resolved to lay siege to Calais. The plan was to turn it into a permanent English enclave on the French coast, a secure point of entry for the invading armies of the future.

The English king cannot have anticipated the ferocious resistance that he would encounter at Calais. The town was powerfully fortified, entirely surrounded by water or marsh, and defended by a large and enthusiastic French garrison. The English army dug itself in around the beleaguered town. A huge military town of timber was built to house the king and his household staff and troops. They were destined to remain there for eleven months.

At first, Philip pinned his hopes upon the Scots. They were persuaded to invade England in force in the hope of compelling Edward to abandon the siege and recross the Channel to defend his realm. Edward knew that the north of England was weakly defended. But he refused to move. The Scots had never penetrated much further south than Newcastle. He resolved to let the Scots do their worst in the northern counties. In the event, the Scots suffered a major and unexpected reverse. After passing Durham, on 17 October 1346, they ran into a large, locally recruited English army commanded by the wardens of the march and the worldly Archbishop of York at Neville's Cross. They were wiped out. The Scottish king, David II, was captured and carried off as a prisoner to London to be paraded through the streets of the city, and then locked in the Tower.

Philip VI did his best to raise an army to relieve Calais. But he was now in serious financial difficulty. There was little appetite among his men for another pitched battle with the English. Less than half the numbers expected turned up at the muster, and by the end of October 1346, the attempt was abandoned. Another attempt at raising an army was made in the following spring. This time the recruiting officers were more successful. But logistical and financial problems meant that the army was not ready to march until July 1347. By this time, the English were in a position of overpowering strength. They had succeeded in blockading Calais on the seaward side, and capturing the Rysbank, a spit of land north of the town which controlled the entrance to the harbour. Fresh troops had been raised in England, bringing the army's strength by the summer of 1347 to about 26,000 men, the largest English army of the whole medieval period. Inside Calais, the defenders were starving. On 27 July 1347, Philip VI appeared on the heights of Sangatte overlooking Calais, with an army of some 15,000 to 20,000 men, more or less comparable to the one which had fought at Crécy. He remained there for four days while his officers tried to work out a way of confronting the vast and well dug-in English army. But the defenders of the town could wait no longer. They signalled that they had had enough. They intended to surrender. The French army marched away, and on 3 August Calais opened its gates to the English.

The surrender of Calais was one of the most celebrated scenes of the Middle Ages and, thanks to Auguste Rodin, the moment of the war which is probably best known to our own age. Six 'burghers of Calais' emerged from the gate in their shirtsleeves with nooses around their necks. They came to the foot of the dais on which Edward, Queen

Philippa and the principal English captains were seated, and threw themselves on the ground begging for mercy. It was the high point of Edward III's career as a soldier. But he was not inclined to be magnanimous. He had been kept out of a town which he called his own for nearly a year. He had with difficulty been persuaded to grant the defenders any terms at all, and had only agreed on terms that these six should be at his mercy. He called for the executioner. All of them, he announced, would be beheaded. He brushed aside the protests of his own captains. It was only when his wife pleaded personally for their lives that, with evident ill-grace, he relented. Calais was destined to remain in English hands for two centuries, a bleak outpost of England, inhabited by a large professional garrison and a population of Englishmen. In September 1347, Edward patched up another temporary truce with the French and returned in triumph to England.

4
Prince of Chivalry
(1347–1360)

It was customary in the courts of Europe to exchange gifts of jewellery at New Year. In 1333, Philippa of Hainault gave her husband a magnificent silver and enamel set of drinking vessels decorated with the arms of England and scenes of war, with castles, warships and armies. In the middle stood Edward himself, surrounded by the great military heroes of legend: Julius Caesar, Judas Maccabeus, Charlemagne, King Arthur, Roland and Oliver, Gawain and Lancelot of the Lake. The gift was well chosen. Edward loved ceremony and show, and relished the symbolism of war. After his assumption of power, he had thrown himself into a succession of spectacular tournaments, in which the participants fought each other in extravagant liveries with exotic badges and devices, such as swans, peacocks and dragons; or disguised as, for example, Tartars, or the pope and his cardinals, or the Seven Deadly Sins. During the king's campaigns in the Low Countries, there were more tournaments in Antwerp, Brussels and Ghent. Pleasure and play-acting were an important part of these occasions, but not the whole. They cemented the bonds between Edward and the English nobility. They provided valuable practical training in horsemanship and weapons-handling when it came to real war. They drew knights-errant to the king's court from continental Europe, many of whom would serve in his armies during the war with France. Above all, they were inspired propaganda.

After the king's victorious return from the siege of Calais, the ceremonial of his court took on a triumphalist tone. At the midsummer tournament at Windsor in June 1348, the participants included the Constable of France, the Chamberlain of Normandy and the King of Scotland, David II, all of them Edward's prisoners, as well as Charles of Blois, the pretender to Brittany who had recently been defeated and captured in the Battle of La Roche-Derrien. That summer, Edward founded the Order of the Garter to commemorate the victory at Crécy. Orders of chivalry were were relatively new in the 1340s. A celebration of nobility and military prowess, dedicated to an idealized notion of knighthood, the Order of the Garter comprised twenty-six members divided into two jousting teams, one of them led by the king and the other by the Prince of Wales. Of the original members, all but two can be shown to have been present at Crécy or in the parallel campaign of Henry of Grosmont in south-western France. The order was dedicated to St George, the archetypal military saint, whom Edward adopted as the patron saint of England. It was on the feast of St George (23 April) that the annual chapters of the order would be held. The order's symbols provoke many questions. Why the garter? Probably because it had been one of the emblems used by the king on the Crécy campaign. What is the meaning of the order's famous motto, *Honi soit qui mal y pense* ('Shame on him who thinks evil of it')? We do not know, but it probably referred to the king's claim to the crown of France, which God had apparently vindicated on the battlefield. At Windsor, the great collegiate chapel of St George shortly began to rise from the ground, part of a general reconstruction of the castle designed to make it the seat of one of the great centres of European chivalry. Over the following decades, indeed centuries, the Order of the Garter became the most famous order of chivalry in Europe, an invaluable tool of royal propaganda and an instrument of patronage both at home and abroad.

The same spirit of adventure and self-aggrandisement, centred on the person of the king, inspired Edward III's next military enterprises.

In December 1349, an Italian adventurer serving in the Calais garrison accepted a large bribe from the French to open the gates of the citadel to their army, and then double-crossed them by reporting the plan to Edward. The king assembled a small army from his own retainers and those who were with him for the Christmas celebrations. A trap was set for the French. The English crossed the Channel in great secrecy by night and lodged themselves in the citadel of Calais. During the night of 1/2 January 1350, the famous French paladin Geoffrey de Charny, accompanied by the principal French commanders of the sector, approached the gate with a force of about 5,000 men. The gate was opened for them and the leading companies lured in. The portcullis closed behind them and they were all captured. Two sorties from the town, one under the king and the other under the Prince of Wales, made short work of the remaining French troops massed on the beach outside.

Some months later, on 29 August, Edward and his son boarded a fleet of requisitioned merchant ships at Sandwich and ambushed some two dozen armed Castilian merchant ships off Winchelsea as they made their way south through the Channel. The Castilians, allies of France who had continued the fight after the proclamation of the truce, had caused havoc in the North Sea earlier in the year, capturing laden English merchant ships and threatening the east coast. Most of the Castilian ships were boarded and captured after a long and bloody fight.

These were brief and colourful interludes in a period when the war with France hung fire. The Black Death, which killed perhaps a third of the population of England and France between 1348 and 1350, initially discouraged the recruitment and movement of large armies. Financial exhaustion paralysed both governments after the exertions of 1345–8. In France, defeat had provoked demoralization and deep political divisions. Large-scale skirmishes continued in Brittany, and frequent dogfights on the march of Gascony. But there were no major continental campaigns.

The main activities of these years were diplomatic. But the forms of diplomacy in the fourteenth century were ill-suited to achieving compromise. They depended on occasional embassies, generally very grand and formal affairs conducted by a bishop and a great nobleman, supported by a team of disputatious clerks with fat volumes of records and memoranda. The proceedings were dominated by wordy speeches, modelled on court sermons and filled with legal and theological argument. These negotiations were more like forensic litigation than any modern diplomatic conference. The participants regarded the ancient quarrel of England and France as something to be resolved by a sustained appeal to authority: in diplomacy the authority of law, and in war that of the God of battles. In this atmosphere, concessions were hard to make. In successive diplomatic exchanges, the French delegates pointed to Edward III's two homages to their king. For the English, this was not the point. Philip VI had refused to recognize Edward's right to the whole of Aquitaine. The God of battles had resolved the issue in his favour at Crécy. Edward was determined to recover the duchy of Aquitaine as it had stood at the accession of his great-grandfather Henry III in 1216. At times he even dreamed of recovering the vast domains of Henry II in the Loire valley and Normandy as well. *Dieu et mon droit.*

Edward III's claim to the crown of France was a bargaining counter, to be surrendered as part of a permanent territorial settlement. Edward always had an exaggerated idea of its value, just as he had an unrealistic view of the strength of his bargaining position generally. He would pass the next decade trying to exploit his victory at Crécy and discovering how much more complicated the world really was. He had won great battles. He had wasted large tracts of France with fire and sword. He had occupied Calais and parts of Brittany, and pushed out the limits of his possessions in the lower Dordogne. But it was obvious that he lacked the means to mount a permanent challenge to the Valois kings in their own territory. Even the Crécy campaign had been no more than a heavy mounted raid by an army which came and then left again. The waves of destruction had crashed over the heads of the French before retreating and leaving people to rebuild their lives. Ancient communities proved to be more resilient than Edward had imagined.

The king might have learned all this from his experience in Scotland. On his return from France in 1347, he appeared to have all the aces in his hand: the shattering victory at Neville's Cross, David II a prisoner in the Tower, Scotland politically divided and demoralized. Gripped by hubris, Edward pitched his demands high. He wanted the overlordship of Scotland, a heavy ransom and the restoration of the dispossessed English lords of southern Scotland. But the Scots simply refused to acknowledge his victory. The Scottish general council and parliament declined to compromise the autonomy of their country, and at first would not even pay a ransom. The Scottish king himself was a chivalrous man, in some ways closer to Edward III than to the lords who dominated the politics of his native land. He was prepared to go further than his subjects in order to obtain his freedom. He made a deal with Edward under which in return for his release one of Edward's sons would succeed him if he failed to produce a direct heir. He was paroled for a few weeks to return to Scotland and persuade his subjects to agree to these terms. But the Scottish parliament would have none of them.

The new King of France, John II, who had succeeded to

the throne on his father's death in 1350, had some things in common with David II. He was chivalrous, but also weak and vacillating. He was also persistently undermined by divisions among the French nobility. In January 1354, John's favourite, Charles of Spain, Constable of France, was murdered at an inn in Normandy by assassins in the service of the king's son-in-law Charles 'the Bad', Count of Evreux and King of Navarre. This incident opened a twenty-year campaign of attrition between this ruthless and cunning politician and the Valois kings of France. After his coup against the constable, Charles the Bad lost no time in making contact with Henry of Grosmont, now Duke of Lancaster, Edward III's principal diplomatic and military adviser, with plans for joint action against John II in France. Actually, Charles had no intention of aligning himself with such a dangerous friend as Edward. But he was perfectly content to flirt with the King of England and for the fact to be known in Paris. It made him a threat to be reckoned with, and raised his bargaining power in the councils of the French king. Faced with two formidable antagonists at once, John's councillors persuaded him that it was necessary to make large concessions to both of them.

In February 1354, the French government bought off the opposition of Charles the Bad with a generous settlement in the town of Mantes on the Seine. Shortly afterwards, a major diplomatic conference opened in the small fortress-town of Guines outside Calais, under the auspices of the manipulative papal legate in France, Guy, Cardinal of Boulogne. In April 1354, a remarkable draft treaty was sealed. John undertook to cede the whole of Aquitaine as it had stood at the accession of Henry III in 1216, together with the Loire provinces of Anjou, Maine and Touraine, all in full sovereignty. The terms were to be ratified at a further conference at the papal court at Avignon in the autumn. The treaty was never ratified. Its authors on the French royal council were overthrown during the summer and replaced by more determined men. When, at the end of the year, the Duke of Lancaster arrived at the papal court at Avignon to see to the ratification and publication of the treaty, he was met with excuses and procrastination. Eventually, the French ambassadors declared that they had no intention of ratifying the draft treaty. Charles the Bad was present in Avignon during the conference, and visited Lancaster in his lodgings. There, the two men resumed their earlier intrigues.

Edward III had always greatly overestimated the help that conspirators and malcontents could bring him. One after another, Robert of Artois, Jacob van Artevelde, John de Montfort and Godfrey of Harcourt had failed him. He never learned from the experience. Charles the Bad would be no different. In the spring of 1355, Edward determined to reopen the war on the most ambitious scale. At the time, his financial position was unusually strong. The more pressing debts of the previous decade had been settled. A parliamentary subsidy was collected every year between 1348 and 1357. The customs service had been expertly reorganized by the indispensable Treasurer, William Eddington, and had become the government's main source of revenue. Aided by a boom in English wool exports, its receipts were more than doubled. The French government by comparison was invitingly weak, its finances in disarray with a civil war threatening.

Against this background, Edward made fresh plans for military intervention. Even more grandiose than the great strategic pincer movement of 1345, they involved the simultaneous deployment of two armies. The Black Prince, now at the age of twenty-four emerging as a notable military commander, was to be sent to Gascony by sea with a glittering company of captains, including no less than nine Knights of the Garter, and more than 2,000 mounted men. A much larger force raised in the duchy itself was to join them at Bordeaux. A second army, about 1,200 strong and including three earls with their retinues, was to sail for Normandy under the command of the Duke of Lancaster. Like the Prince of Wales, Lancaster was counting on being able to recruit the bulk of his forces in France, among the allies of Charles the Bad. The idea was to force the French to divide their strength between two fronts and then, if possible, to defeat them in detail.

Things quickly began to go wrong. Charles the Bad double-crossed his English allies and made a separate peace with John II in September 1355, as he had always intended to do. At the time, the Duke of Lancaster and the Black Prince were both at sea with their armies. Lancaster, who had been delayed by adverse winds, was recalled in time. The Black Prince sailed on to Bordeaux, but with the northern arm of the English pincer abandoned, the French were free to turn their whole strength against him. In England, Edward III panicked. He had not originally intended to fight in France himself. But some way had to be found of mounting a diversion in order to draw off the French army in the north and prevent it from concentrating against the Prince in Gascony. So, in October, Edward sailed for Calais with the ships and troops which had been raised for the abortive campaign in Normandy. From here, he mounted a destructive raid into the French province of Picardy.

Edward's *chevauchée* was enough to make the French king cancel his plans for a campaign against the Black Prince on the march of Gascony. But it contributed very little to the English king's honour or his bargaining power. In Edward's absence the Scots had invaded the north of England with the support of a small but highly profes-sional French expeditionary force, and had recaptured Berwick-on-Tweed, the largest English fortress of the bor-der. As a result, Edward was forced to scurry back to England with his army after a mere ten days in the field. By Christmas Eve, the king was at Newcastle. In January, Berwick was retaken, and the next six weeks were occupied in wasting southern Scotland.

In the event, it was the campaigns of the Prince which were to transform the political situation. Between September and December 1355, he conducted a bold mounted raid nearly 300 miles across southern France from Bordeaux on the Atlantic coast to Narbonne on the Mediterranean and back again. The object was destruction, just as his father's had been in Picardy and Scotland. No battles were won. No territory was conquered. But at least a dozen walled towns and 500 open villages lay in ruins. The army returned to the Gironde with a thousand wagons of booty. This no doubt raised morale among the Gascons and eased recruitment for the next campaign. There are glimpses of a wider strategy. At Carcassonne, the Prince's officials examined tax records and interrogated officials about the economy of the region. They thought that the devastation wrought by the Prince had reduced the taxable capacity of Languedoc by 400,000 *écus* a year. Modern research suggests that this figure may well be about right. At Westminster, Edward III received the news of his son's operations in the New Year and began to lay plans for exploiting them. The old dream of simultaneous campaigns in north and south was revived. Reinforcements sailed for Gascony from Plymouth as soon as the winter gales were over. A small seaborne expedition was ordered to sail from Southampton for Brittany in the spring under the command of the Duke of Lancaster.

It was at this critical juncture that the French response was crippled by a major political crisis. For some weeks, there had been persistent rumours of a plot by Charles the Bad to seize power with the aid of his allies among the nobility of Normandy. It was even rumoured that the plotters included John II's heir, the Dauphin, Charles. On 5 April 1356, the Dauphin was presiding at a banquet in the great hall of Rouen Castle. The King of Navarre and most of his Norman allies were present. Without warning, the door opened and the King of France entered in full armour accompanied by a troop of soldiers. Charles the Bad was arrested and sent off under guard to Paris. Four of his chief confederates, including the head of the leading noble house of Normandy, were summarily executed. Over the following weeks, as Edward III's army was gathering in Southampton, John II's troops were heavily engaged in Normandy besieging the strongholds of Charles the Bad and his allies. The leadership of the Navarrese cause was taken up by Charles's brother Philip. His first act was to send agents to England to make common cause with the invaders.

Edward seized with both hands the opportunity offered by the French civil war. Lancaster's fleet, which was almost ready to sail, was diverted from Brittany to Normandy. Arrangements were hurriedly made to embark a Navarrese army in Bayonne and carry it to Normandy in Gascon ships. Across central and southern England and the march of Wales, troops were raised to accompany Edward himself to France. Using Normandy as a base, he intended to join forces with the Black Prince in the Loire valley and confront John II with their combined force.

These plans were frustrated by a combination of misfortune and shrewd French countermeasures. At the beginning of August 1356, the Black Prince marched north from Bergerac on the Dordogne, making for the Loire. He had about 6,000 men under his command, about a third of them English, the rest Gascon. But as the Prince began his march, a galley fleet supplied by France's Aragonese allies arrived in the Seine. They were sent forward to harry the south coast of England, and within a week were sighted off Kent. Fearing for the security of his kingdom and unwilling to risk his army in an encounter with the galleys in the Channel, Edward III cancelled his plans to go to France. The Duke of Lancaster was in Normandy. He was directed

1. Edward III doing homage to Philip VI of France, 'hands between hands', in Amiens Cathedral, 6 June 1329.

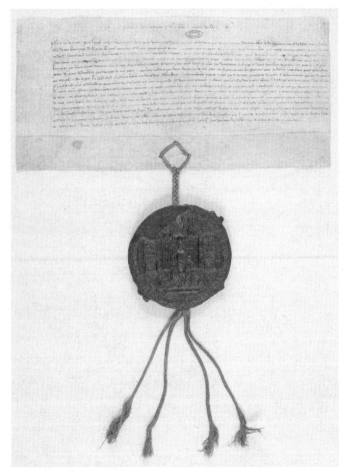

2. Edward III challenges Philip VI to try their claims to the crown of France by single combat, 26 July 1340. The challenge is sealed with the King's Great Seal.

3. The naval battle of Sluys, 24 June 1340, from a manuscript of Froissart's *Chronicles*. The battle destroyed France's naval power for a generation.

4. Edward III's gold noble, first issued in 1344. 'Four things our noble showeth to me,' wrote a fifteenth-century Englishman, 'King, ship and sword, and power of the sea.'

5. Crossing the Seine at Poissy, 14 August 1346. From here, Edward III marched north to Crécy and Calais.

6. The Battle of Crécy, 26 August 1346. Edward III's most famous victory made his reputation in the eyes of contemporaries.

7. Edward III and King David of Scotland in 1357.
Captured in battle in 1346, David was Edward's prisoner
for eleven years.

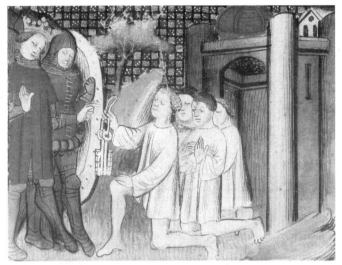

8. The surrender of Calais, 3 August 1347, after a siege of eleven months. For two centuries, Calais would be England's principal bastion in France.

9. Hadleigh Castle, overlooking the Thames estuary from the Essex coast, as Constable painted it in 1829. It was built after the Treaty of Brétigny (1360) to defend London in the next French war.

10. Tomb effigy of Bertrand du Guesclin, Constable of France, in the Abbey of Saint-Denis. His shrewd strategic judgement turned the tide of war against the English.

11. Tomb effigy of Philippa of Hainault, Queen of England, in Westminster Abbey. With her death in 1369 began Edward's long descent into senility.

12. Tomb effigy of Edward, the Black Prince, in Canterbury Cathedral. 'On his death,' wrote the chronicler Thomas Walsingham, 'the hopes of England utterly perished.'

13. Detail of Edward III from the Great Charter of Bristol (1373). Bristol was already one of the centres of English maritime power.

14. Benjamin West, *The Burghers of Calais* (1789), painted for the audience chamber of George III at Windsor Castle, was one of a series commemorating the founder members of the Order of the Garter.

to join forces with the Black Prince in the king's place. As soon as he received these orders, Lancaster set out for the Loire with about 2,400 English troops. Shortly afterwards, the Prince reached the Loire at Tours. But the French had secured all the crossings of the river, thus preventing the junction of the two English armies. Unable to join forces with the Prince and heavily outnumbered by the army of the French king, Lancaster returned empty-handed to Normandy.

In the middle of September 1356, John II crossed the Loire, and set out in pursuit of the Black Prince at the head of an army nearly twice as strong as his. The Prince did not rate his chances of overcoming the enemy in the face of odds like these. He turned back towards Bordeaux, hoping to avoid battle. But his army was slowed down by their heavy baggage train. The French van overtook them and cut them off east of Poitiers, leaving the Prince with little choice but to fight.

Edward III had set these events in motion, but the cancellation of his own expedition left him to follow the outcome from England, separated from his armies by distances that took at least a fortnight for a fast messenger to cover. At about the beginning of October, the silence was broken. A messenger from Cherbourg landed in England with the news of a great battle near Poitiers two weeks before. The French army had been routed. The King of France and one of his sons had been taken prisoner, along with many of his leading captains and councillors. A few days later, one of the Black Prince's servants arrived at the English court with confirmation and trophies: John II's helmet and his tunic embroidered with the arms of France. Meanwhile, the Black Prince had returned in triumph to Bordeaux with the spoil and prisoners. In the following year, they took ship for England. On 24 May 1357, eight months after the battle, the Prince made his entry into London. John II was prominent among the prisoners following in the victor's wake. He was installed in courteous captivity with a miniature court in exile in the great palace of the Savoy on the Strand, which Henry of Grosmont had built a decade before from the spoils of his campaign in Gascony. 'The Pope is a Frenchman, but Jesus is an Englishman,' wrote an English chronicler; 'now we shall discover which is stronger.'[1]

'We take no pleasure in the slaughter of men,' Edward wrote in a circular to the bishops designed to be read out from pulpits, 'but we rejoice in God's bounty and we look forward to a just and early peace.'[2] Peace would come one day. But it would not be early or just, according to most people's lights. On the face of it, Edward III was in a position of overpowering strength. He and his lieutenants had twice destroyed French royal armies substantially larger than their own. His two principal antagonists, the Kings of France and Scotland, were both prisoners in London. Charles of Blois, the royalist candidate to the ducal throne of Brittany, had by now agreed to humiliating terms, promising an enormous ransom and prevented by the legal convention of the day from fighting for his own cause until the last instalment had been paid. Edward would shortly agree very similar terms with the Scots.

Meanwhile, France descended into chaos. The Duke

of Lancaster occupied a string of fortresses on the south-western march of Normandy and installed permanent garrisons in them. The English and Navarrese armies in Normandy fragmented into self-governing 'free companies'. They spread east, roaming across the great plains of northern France, while, in the south, bands of Gascon brigands moved up the river valleys into the central highlands and from there to the valleys of the Rhone and the Saône, capturing one fortress after another. There was very little resistance. The French treasury was empty. The tax system collapsed. In Paris, the Dauphin was nominally in control as his father's lieutenant. Real power quickly passed into the hands of cabals of ambitious politicians.

John II's consuming desire was to be released, and it soon became obvious that he was prepared to concede almost anything. But, isolated in Bordeaux and then in London, the French king was out of touch with his subjects. They had other priorities. When, a month after the battle, the Estates-General met in Paris, they showed no interest in authorizing taxes to ransom their king. They voted taxes, but reserved them for war. They elected a council of eighty to serve as a provisional government. It was dominated by inveterate enemies of John II who were determined to carry on the fight. Then, at the end of 1357, Charles the Bad escaped from the prison to which John II had consigned him and made his way to Paris. Together with the Parisian demagogue Etienne Marcel, he set up a revolutionary government which took control of the capital and the northern cities. For these men, the king's absence was not misfortune to be lamented. It was an opportunity to be seized.

In the autumn of 1357, Edward III held a great diplomatic conference with the King of France and his exiled court in London. John's ministers, most of them prisoners like himself, promised an immense ransom of 4 million *écus*, equivalent to several years' revenue and far more than his ruined kingdom could afford. He promised to cede Calais and the whole of the ancient duchy of Aquitaine as it had stood in the time of Eleanor and Henry II two centuries before, about a quarter of the territory of the French kingdom. These vast domains were to be severed from the French crown and held by the King of England in full sovereignty for ever. The terms were finalized at Windsor in April 1358, where the hapless French king was a guest at the annual feast of the Order of the Garter. It was a famous occasion. Heralds had been sent to summon knights from across Europe. Many of Edward's Gascon subjects were there. The festivities were of unparalleled splendour. Even John II, no stranger to extravagance, was reported to have remarked tartly that Edward had a great deal of gold and silver plate for a man so heavily in debt.

In chess, the capture of the king marks the end of the game. In politics, it may be only the beginning. Edward III never really understood the complex political situation in France. He simply assumed that John's assent would be enough. But John's subjects had not been consulted. When the text was brought to Paris by the king's emissaries, the Dauphin's council accepted the terms. But they were repudiated by the city of Paris and then by the Estates-General and much of the country. The Dauphin did his best to force the treaty on his father's subjects. But in February 1358 the Paris mob invaded the royal palace, battered his ministers to death before his eyes and flung their corpses from an upper window. Finally, the Dauphin was forced to withdraw from Paris, leaving the city in the power of Etienne Marcel and Charles the Bad. By the summer of 1358, the revolutionaries were hiring the English free companies to prop up their regime in the capital. Beyond the walls, a violent peasant uprising, the Jacquerie, destroyed crops and barns and burned manors across the Ile de France. It was not until August 1358, after the Parisians had turned against the revolution and Etienne Marcel had been lynched in the streets, that the Dauphin succeeded in recovering a measure of control over the capital. But he had learned the lessons of the past months. He abandoned the attempt to impose the terms of peace agreed by his father. Frustrated and angry, Edward III finally repudiated the treaty in November 1358, and announced his intention of mounting a fresh invasion of France in the following year. In the meantime, the old courtesies between kings were abandoned. Orders were given to remove John from the comfort of the Savoy Palace to the austere moated castle of Somerton in Lincolnshire.

The King of France and the group of exiles around him in London panicked. They believed that unless peace was made with Edward III he would make common cause with Charles the Bad. To avoid this calamity, they capitulated to all the English demands. A new treaty was drawn up in the city in February 1359 after just three weeks of negotiation. It ceded to Edward not only Calais and an enlarged duchy of Aquitaine but Normandy, Brittany and Maine, and the provinces of Anjou and Touraine in the western Loire, nearly half the territory of France.

If the Treaty of Windsor was unacceptable to the French, there was little prospect of their accepting the even more craven terms of the Treaty of London. It soon began to dawn on Edward that he would never be able to exploit his possession of the King of France until John's authority in his realm had been restored. The main impediment to this was the operations of his sometime ally Charles the Bad and of his own subjects, English or Gascon, serving with the free companies. The true costs of the policy of terror were now coming home to him. True, the disorder in France had disabled it from fighting an effective war, but the chaos was now making it impossible to agree upon an effective peace. Too late, he tried to prop up his royal prisoner's position in France. He sent agents across the Channel with orders for his subjects to return to their castles. He rejected the King of Navarre's offers of co-operation. He released on parole some of John's leading associates in London and allowed them to return to Paris. Finally, he postponed the planned invasion until June 1359 to allow time for them to take control of the French government in Paris and impose the new treaty on his subjects.

It was all to no avail. Edward's new tack might have worked if his demands had not been so extravagant. But when John II's companions arrived in Paris they found that there was no support for the treaty that he had signed. In May 1359, a poorly attended session of the Estates-General dismissed it as 'impossible, unacceptable'. When the news of its rejection reached England, Edward reinstated the invasion plans which he had put on hold in February. He planned to land with a large army at Calais and fight his way across northern France to the city of Reims, the traditional coronation city of the kings of France. There, he probably intended to have himself crowned as King of France. Edward III landed at Calais at the end of October 1359, with an army of about 10,000 men. He was accompanied by most of the famous captains who had fought his wars since his first campaigns in Scotland a quarter of a century before. The army set out from Calais in three columns, commanded by Edward himself, the Black Prince and the Duke of Lancaster.

The French defence was conducted by the Dauphin. After two shattering defeats in the field, his captains adopted a new strategy. It was, with some variants, the strategy which the French would follow for the next half-century. It was simple, cheap and highly effective. They abandoned the open country, retreating into the walled towns and castles. They took with them all the stores that they could carry and destroyed whatever had to be left behind. Detachments of mounted men followed the route of the English army at a distance, refusing battle but picking off stragglers and making it all but impossible for the invaders to forage. As a result, the English began to experience severe hardship only a few days into the campaign. The winter was to be the worst for many years. Torrential rain soaked the men to the skin, and turned the roads into marshes. The rivers were black with mud and debris, and the water undrinkable. Supplies of food and fodder ran out.

Early in December, after a month on the road, the English army arrived outside Reims. The French, who had advance warning from spies of Edward's intentions, had put the city in a state of defence. Its stores were full. The walls bristled with men and guns. The English rapidly consumed all the stores to be had in the area, and had to forage over ever greater distances to find food. The foragers suffered heavy casualties. In January 1360, after a siege of five weeks, Edward marched away. His failure before Reims left his army with no discernible strategy. The king extracted a large ransom in return for leaving the duchy of Burgundy alone. Thereafter, the campaign deteriorated into a large-scale pillaging expedition. Edward marched his army round the south side of Paris, destroying everything in his path. In the second week of April, they arrived outside the southern ramparts of Paris. They marched back and forth outside the capital, burning suburbs and villages in the hope of drawing the French into battle. But they were not to be drawn. Finally, unable to find supplies in the Paris region, they withdrew west into the Beauce through the sleet and rain. As they approached Chartres, the temperature fell. A great thunderstorm was followed by hail. Carts full of equipment and booty sank into the mud and had to be abandoned. Starvation, disease and exposure claimed men in their hundreds.

It was the Duke of Lancaster who persuaded Edward that he could not go on. Jean Froissart attributed to him words which summed up the king's predicament, whether or not he ever spoke them:

> Sir, you are waging a tremendous war in France, and fortune has so far favoured you. But it is your subjects who are making money out of it, while you are just marking time. You now have a choice. You can press on with the struggle and spend the rest of your life fighting. Or you can make terms when you can still come out of it with honour. My advice is to accept the offers that have already been made to you. You know perfectly well that you could lose in one day everything that you have gained in twenty years.[3]

The negotiations were conducted in the tiny hamlet of Brétigny, outside Chartres. Once it became clear that Edward was no longer insisting on the extravagant terms imposed on John II in the Treaty of London, the diplomats made rapid progress. After just three days of talks, a draft treaty was prepared on substantially the same terms as the abortive Treaty of Windsor which Edward had repudiated eighteen months before. Edward was to renounce his claim to the crown of France. In return he would receive the enlarged duchy of Aquitaine, as it had stood at the beginning of the thirteenth century, the town and district of Calais and the county of Ponthieu, all in full sovereignty. In addition, a ransom of 3 million *écus* would be payable in instalments over a period of six years. While the instalments were being paid, John would be released on parole, in return for twenty-five hostages selected from the highest noblemen of France, including the French king's three younger sons, and representatives of all the main towns. It was a remarkable diplomatic achievement, given the weakness of Edward's position. Left to himself, the Dauphin would have preferred to wait for the bedraggled English army to abandon the fight and return home. But the French negotiators were receiving their instructions from John II's representatives in Paris, not the Dauphin. They were determined to get their master out of his English prison on the best terms available. On 19 May 1360, Edward III embarked for England at Honfleur in the Seine estuary. His army, looking for all the world like a defeated rabble, trudged through Picardy to take ship from Calais.

John II was released at Calais in October 1360 at a formal ceremony in the presence of both kings and their principal advisers, as soon as the first instalment of the ransom had been counted out, assayed by goldsmiths and confirmed by accountants. A number of details which had been left open at Brétigny were resolved while all this was happening. For the most part, the terms were confirmed without changes. But Edward, who may well have felt that he had been pushed into agreeing terms at Brétigny, was pathologically suspicious of the French. He regarded his claim to the French throne, which he had promised to renounce, as his only effective means of ensuring that they complied with the treaty. This view is hard to justify and may not have been shared by his advisers. But it led him to insist that his renunciation of his claim should be postponed until after the ceded provinces had been delivered up to his representatives. The French responded that in that case, although the process of transferring the ceded provinces to English rule would go ahead as planned, John II would retain nominal sovereignty over them until Edward had abandoned his claim to the throne, but would promise not to exercise it. Accordingly, the two renunciations were taken out of the main treaty and inserted into a side-letter. This provided that both renunciations should be performed simultaneously at some stage before November 1361. The side-letter became known as the *clause c'estassavoir* ('that is to say'), after its opening word. It was a fatal mistake. Although no one at Calais foresaw it, this apparently innocuous amendment to the timing would one day unravel the whole agreement.

5
Decline and Fall
(1360–1377)

On 13 November 1362, Edward III's fiftieth birthday, his jubilee was celebrated in a magnificent ceremony at Westminster. He had been on the throne for thirty-five years, longer than any of his forbears except for Henry III. Edward's prestige, already high after the victories of Crécy and Poitiers, had reached its apogee. In the eyes of the rest of Europe, the Treaty of Brétigny was the triumphant conclusion of three decades devoted to war and diplomacy. His court became the most famous centre of chivalry in Europe. The cost of the royal household rose to unprecedented levels. The spectacle was accompanied by a self-conscious emphasis on the Englishness of England, a country traditionally ruled by a francophone dynasty and aristocracy which had once looked for its inspiration to the dominant culture of France. The court now became a centre of patronage for poets writing in English, including the youthful Geoffrey Chaucer. Edward sedulously encouraged the indigenous cults of St George and King Arthur.

Yet the splendour of Westminster and Windsor in these years was built on shallow foundations. The immense cost was funded by one-off windfalls, mainly the instalments of the ransoms of Burgundy, John II, David of Scotland and Charles of Blois. Like his captains, Edward regarded these as his private income, and had them paid into a personal treasury reserved for his own use, thus enabling him for a few years to live well beyond his income. Yet outside the court, the future seemed uncertain. Edward's victories in France had been made possible by the divisions of his enemies, which would one day heal. As for the treaty, that had been imposed by John II on the French political community in order to regain his liberty. Its fulfilment depended mainly on the French king's sense of honour and personal commitment, which were strong but not shared by his heir, the Dauphin, Charles, or by the rest of France. Even Edward was unsure. He built the fortresses of Hadleigh and Queenborough in the Thames estuary as a precaution against future French attacks, and reinforced the defences of Calais and Ponthieu.

Edward's feeling of insecurity was justified, for the treaty quickly turned to dust in his hands. The formal transfer of the ceded territories started late and took longer than anticipated. As the deadline for the renunciations approached, John II pressed for them to be made in advance of the last transfers. Edward would have been wise to agree. But, ever distrustful of the French, he would not. Once the deadline had passed, there was a loose understanding that the terms would be amended to allow the renunciations to be made later. In the event, they never were. Again, this was Edward's own decision. John II and the pope both pressed him to allow the renunciations to be made. But there were still a number of disputes about territory to be resolved. Edward stopped calling himself King of France, but until everything else was settled to his satisfaction he would not formally renounce the title.

Meanwhile, the English found themselves unable to perform their own treaty obligations. In 1360, there were at least 150 castles in the provinces retained by John II which were garrisoned in the name of Edward III. Many thousands of English and Gascon troops were scattered across France, serving in free companies and garrisons. They were making their living in the only way they knew, by plundering the roads and towns, occupying castles and holding whole regions to ransom. Thousands more came to join them from Béarn, Savoy, Brittany, Germany, the Low Countries and above all from England, all of them regions where the peace had left behind a reservoir of unemployed soldiery in need of work. At first, Edward tried to rein in his subjects. A few prominent captains were even arrested and shut in the Tower of London. But except for a small number of Englishmen who were vulnerable on account of their lands and offices in England, the soldiers fighting with the free companies ignored him. Shortly, the English king gave up the attempt and let things take their violent course.

The weakened institutions of the Valois monarchy were overwhelmed. In March 1362, a French army several thousand strong, commanded by the Chamberlain of France, was defeated in a pitched battle at Brignais near Lyons by a coalition of free companies. Over the following years, marauding armies of *routiers* roamed across Languedoc and Auvergne, eventually penetrating into the Loire valley and the march of Normandy. Charles the Bad returned to his old projects, hoping to profit by the anarchy in France to plot the downfall of his Valois rival. He took many of the English and Gascon free companies into his service. To the French, it looked like the continuation of the war by other means.

The ransom of John II quickly fell into arrears. The first instalment had been raised only by selling the king's daughter to the despot of Milan as a bride for his young son in return for an enormous dowry. Expedients like that could not be repeated year after year. Further instalments would have to be funded from taxation. John began the task of rebuilding the shattered tax system of his realm. But it was a long process. The operations of the free companies made it longer still, disrupting collection and forcing the provincial authorities to divert large sums from the ransom treasurers to local defence. The French king's son Louis, Duke of Anjou began to fear that he would waste his entire youth in captivity. He obtained parole to return to France for a short visit, and refused to return.

In January 1364, the King of France travelled to London. His reasons were characteristic of the man. He had ordered Louis of Anjou to return to England, and been met with sullen defiance. So he resolved to stand in for him himself. He hoped that the gesture would enable him to use his personal rapport with Edward III to resolve all the outstanding issues. For some six weeks the French king's staff negotiated with the royal council at Westminster. It was the last occasion on which a durable peace might have been made. But before anything could be agreed, John sickened with the plague that was then endemic in London. On 8 April 1364, he died in his quarters in the Savoy Palace. He was succeeded by the Dauphin, Charles.

'You will find the new King a good friend and brother, a man to nourish your goodwill and honour the peace,' one of John II's ministers wrote to Edward III after his death.[1] The author of these words was a poor prophet. The death of John II was a disaster for Edward, for the new king proved to be a very different and less tractable adversary. Twenty-six years old at his accession, Charles V never cut the classic figure of a king. He was physically weak, a poor soldier, an intellectual who kept away from the public gaze. But he was a ruthless and a skilful politician whose choice of subordinates more than made up for his personal disabilities. Charles had never thought well of the compromises which his father had made in order to escape his English prison. He had had no part in making the Treaty of Brétigny, and if the indiscretions of his secretary are to be believed, he had always intended to undo it. According to this man, the new king's first priority was to destroy the power of Charles the Bad in Normandy and of the Montforts in Brittany. Then he would negotiate the return of the principal hostages still in England. When that had been done, he would recover the territory ceded to the English in Aquitaine and 'finally destroy them'.[2] Charles understood better than his father or his adversary that the chief material of war was money. The key to achieving this programme was the rebuilding of the French tax system. The temporary taxes which his father had imposed to pay his ransom now became permanent. The machinery of collection was overhauled. Within five years of his accession the French government had recovered all of its old authority and had achieved a financial position sounder than that of any of its predecessors.

Edward III's main ambition in these years was to find principalities for his five surviving sons, both in the British Isles, where they would serve as instruments for subordinating all of Britain to the English dynasty, and in western Europe, where they would cement a ring of alliances encircling France and protect him against the revival of French military power. He had made the Black Prince Duke of Cornwall in 1337, the first time that this title had been used in England. In 1362, two new dukedoms were created: Clarence for his second son, Lionel; and Lancaster for his third son, John of Gaunt. Lionel was married to the daughter of Gian Galazzo Visconti, despot of Milan, with a generous territorial settlement in northern Italy. The king returned to the old project of diverting the succession to the throne of Scotland to John of Gaunt. For the fourth son, Edmund Langley, an even more dazzling future was planned. In October 1364, a treaty was made with Louis de Mâle, Count of Flanders, under which Edmund was to marry his daughter Margaret. Margaret was the greatest heiress of Europe, the designated ruler after her father's death of Flanders, Brabant, Limburg and the imperial county of Burgundy. Under the terms of the treaty, Edmund would become the ruler of all of these domains on France's northern and eastern flank. In addition, he would have settled on him Calais and its surrounding territory, Ponthieu, and his mother's claim to a share in the succession to

Hainault. All of these territories were to be held by him as fiefs of the English crown.

In the end nothing came of these great projects. Lionel died within a few weeks of his marriage to Violante Visconti, poisoned, as the English believed. The Scots refused to accept Edward's plans for the succession to David II, as they always had done. And the plan to marry Edmund to Margaret of Flanders was frustrated by the French pope. At the request of Charles V, he refused to grant the dispensation which was required by canon law for any marriage between persons with a common ancestor within seven generations. Instead, Margaret was married in 1368 to Charles V's younger brother Philip, Duke of Burgundy, thus laying the foundation for the great Franco-Burgundian empire in the Low Countries in the fifteenth century. Philip was just as closely related to Margaret as Edmund, but in his case the dispensation was forthcoming at once. The whole affair was symptomatic of the recovery of French influence and prestige during the 1360s.

Of all Edward III's children, it was the Black Prince who was to achieve the highest fortune and suffer the greatest fall. In 1362, the king had made the enlarged duchy of Aquitaine into an autonomous principality under the English crown, and conferred it on the Prince. The new ruler of Aquitaine arrived in the territory with 700 English troops, and established a court which for a few years outshone even his father's. 'And they all loved him and honoured him as their lord,' wrote Froissart, 'and proclaimed his principality to be the greatest in the world and the richest in valiant men-at-arms.'[3] But although the

Prince was a skilful military commander, he proved to be a tactless and authoritarian ruler and a financially incontinent administrator, whose want of political judgement was only partly made good by his advisers. His desire to cut a great figure on a European scale quickly caused problems. He quarrelled with his Gascon subjects. He embroiled the English in unnecessary quarrels with the French government. He supported Charles the Bad's attempt to recover his confiscated domains in Normandy, allowing him to recruit English and Gascon troops in his lands. He sent an army to intervene on the side of the Montforts in Brittany. This assertiveness was expensive. The size of the Prince's household and military retinue, coming on top of the cost of governing and defending the vast territory of Aquitaine, made it necessary to introduce a system of local taxation far more onerous than the region had known before.

In 1366, the Black Prince resolved to intervene in the civil war in Castile in support of King Pedro, an ally of England who was fighting for his throne against his French-backed half-brother Henry of Trastámara. The campaign was a military triumph but a political disaster. Henry and his partly French army were decisively defeated in April 1367 at the Battle of Nájera east of Burgos, perhaps the Prince's greatest moment as a military commander. Pedro was restored to his throne and Henry of Trastámara forced to flee to France. But the cost of the Prince's expedition was many times the income of his domains. Most of his army was serving on credit. Pedro had promised to reimburse his expenses and to cede much of the Basque

Country to him. But the Castilian king was neither able nor willing to perform these undertakings. When the Prince recrossed the Pyrenees in September 1367, he was sick and bankrupt. As for Pedro, he survived on his throne for only two years until Henry of Trastámara murdered him and assumed power with the support of another French army.

In order to pay off the debts generated by the Castilian adventure, the Black Prince instituted a permanent hearth tax, essentially a tax on every household. He obtained the consent of a poorly attended meeting of the Estates of his principality. But the tax was profoundly unpopular and widely resisted. The resistance was led by the most powerful territorial magnates of the south-west, John, Count of Armagnac and his ally the Lord of Albret. They appealed against the hearth tax to the Parlement of Paris, the highest court of France. Behind the scenes, Charles V had encouraged the appellants, plying them with favours and money. And when they lodged their appeal, he accepted it. It was a direct challenge to the Brétigny settlement. Under the terms of the treaty, the King of France had promised that he would not exercise sovereignty in Aquitaine even if sovereignty had not been formally renounced. But Charles's lawyers argued that this promise was void. If sovereignty had not been renounced, he was duty bound to exercise it. Besides, they added, the failure of Edward III and his son to control their subjects fighting with the free companies was a repudiation of the treaty. The French king was therefore no longer bound by it. The Black Prince was summoned to answer the appeal before the Parlement. This effectively reduced him to the status of a vassal of France. In May 1369, he was declared in default, and in due course Aquitaine was formally confiscated. Edward III responded by resuming the title of King of France. The breach was complete.

The Prince reacted with fury to Charles V's summons. He would answer it, he said, with a helmet on his head and an army at his back. But this was just bravado. The Prince had returned from Castile with a debilitating illness from which he would suffer intermittently for the rest of his life. For long periods he was bedridden or unable to attend to business. He became ill-tempered and less inclined to listen to advice. His court lost the glamour which had drawn so many men to his service. His subordinates included some able men, who did what they could to defend his principality against the French. But it was not much. Within eighteen months, the French king's brother Louis, Duke of Anjou had overrun most of the new provinces of Aquitaine south of the Dordogne. Another brother, John, Duke of Berry, invaded the Limousin on the eastern march of the principality in 1370. In August 1370, the Black Prince gathered an army and, carried by bearers in a litter, led them against the city of Limoges, which had just followed the example of so many others and opened its gates to the French. The city was taken by storm. Froissart's exaggerated account of the slaughter which followed is perhaps the blackest mark against the Prince's reputation. Its real importance was that it was his last campaign. Pausing at Cognac on his way back, he announced his intention to abandon the government of Aquitaine to his younger brother John of Gaunt, Duke of Lancaster. In the following spring, he returned to England a broken man.

Edward III was the impotent spectator of these events. He was fifty-six years old when Charles V of France repudiated the treaty, an old man by medieval standards. The clouds had been gathering over his head since 1364. His household expenditure began to fall, a sign of returning financial stringency after years of carefree spectacle and largesse. He began to suffer from periodic health problems. He gave up jousting and hunting, while his household accounts reveal a rising consumption of medicines and the frequent attendance of doctors. According to Froissart, when Peter of Cyprus asked him to join a crusade in 1364, the king replied that he was too old for all that now and would rather leave such adventures to his sons. The queen, Philippa of Hainault, died in August 1369. Thereafter, Edward increasingly withdrew from public view, spending much of his time at the royal manors of Havering, Eltham and Sheen. On his rare visits to the great public palaces of Westminster and Windsor, he preferred to remain secluded in his chamber, away from the noise and gossip of the hall.

Edward had outlived the friends and companions of his youth and authors of his victories. The six earls that he had created in 1337 on the eve of his great war with France were all dead. Henry of Grosmont, the wisest and most influential of them, had died in 1361 not long after the Treaty of Brétigny. William Eddington, whose skilful management of Edward's finances had been a major factor in the triumphs of the 1350s, retired two years later in

1363. The government passed into the hands of a new generation of men who lacked their predecessors' political skills: the king's third son, John of Gaunt; his impetuous son-in-law John Hastings, Earl of Pembroke; the corrupt William Latimer, a soldier of fortune who had made his way in Brittany; and (until his dismissal in 1371) the manipulative and all-powerful chancellor, William of Wykeham. In his prime, the king's companionable personality and his judicious use of patronage had enabled him to muster support for his wars among men of very varied interests and temperament. His relative inaccessibility in the 1370s and the diversion of royal favour to a clique of greedy cronies brought an end to all that.

Edward III was not the first English king to take a mistress and would certainly not be the last. But Alice Perrers, his only recorded extra-marital liaison, was unique among royal mistresses of the Middle Ages. She had caught the king's eye in the early 1360s, when she was a lady-in-waiting to the queen, and in 1364 bore him a son, shortly followed by two daughters. The relationship remained discreet while Philippa was alive, but after her death Alice emerged from the shadows. She was brazen, greedy and pushy, with her own protégés to promote and her own ambitions to pursue. She used her influence with the king to extract money from the royal coffers, between £2,000 and £3,000 a year, according to plausible estimates in Parliament. She played a prominent and highly visible role at court and on public occasions. She also proved to be a shrewd businesswoman, forging links with city financiers, trading her influence for riches and accumulating substantial wealth. As a result, she was heartily detested, and her unpopularity rubbed off on the king.

The 1370s were a difficult time in England. Persistent outbreaks of bubonic plague and cattle murrain weakened the economy. International wool prices, on which much of the English economy and the public finances depended, were low. Parliamentary opinion was no longer behind the war in the way it had once been. The public cared about the Scottish border and the security of southern England against French raids. They cared too about the defence of Calais, which had become the chief entrepôt for cross-Channel trade and virtually an outpost of the business community of London. But the quiescence of the Scots and divisions of France under John II had removed the fears which had made Edward's wars popular. The English found it hard to muster much enthusiasm for the defence of Edward III's possessions in south-western France. They were widely regarded as his personal affair. As a result, the government did not dare to approach Parliament for war taxes in the aftermath of Charles V's repudiation of the treaty. Instead, the war was funded mainly from the king's personal treasury and without recourse to parliamentary taxation. The king took no personal part in the fighting. He abandoned a plan to lead a major raid into Picardy in 1369, the first of many abortive schemes to return to his old life in the saddle. The task was delegated to John of Gaunt and a reliable veteran, the Earl of Warwick.

By 1370, Edward had run out of money. Serious difficulties were encountered over the following years in persuading Parliament to vote subsidies for a war that no longer seemed to serve any specifically English purpose. The king and his ministers were finally forced to confront the fact that they were facing a skilful and determined antagonist with far greater resources than their own. They tried to revive the strategies of the 1350s, but found that they no longer worked. An attempt was made to rekindle the civil wars of France by bringing Charles the Bad back to Normandy. But the Navarrese ruler was outmanoeuvred by Charles V's ministers and captains, and his final attempt to make war on his Valois cousins was snuffed out. The English established links with the diminished remnants of the free companies in northern France. A powerful campaign was organized in 1370 under the command of the old freebooter Sir Robert Knolles. Funded as a large-scale plundering venture, it was ultimately wiped out at the Battle of Pontvallain in December 1370.

For Edward personally, the crunch came in 1372. The French, having driven the English from most of the newly ceded provinces of Aquitaine lying south of the Dordogne, now resolved to concentrate their strength against the provinces further north. These regions were the economic and military heart of the principality. The campaign was conducted by the new Constable of France, Bertrand du Guesclin, an inspired strategist with a shrewd eye for weaknesses of the English territories. The English council, which was well aware of the French intentions, devised an ambitious counterstroke, reminiscent of the pincer movement of 1356. The Earl of Pembroke was to sail for Gascony with chests of silver with which to raise an army in Aquitaine. Edward III himself was to lead an army of

6,000 Englishmen to Brittany. The two armies were to join forces in the Loire valley and confront the French army together.

The plan was a humiliating failure. Pembroke's fleet was intercepted off La Rochelle by a galley fleet sent by France's Castilian ally, Henry of Trastámara. Pembroke himself was captured, together with his silver. The king's expedition was crippled by constant postponements and changes of plan, the result of a shortage of shipping, Castilian naval operations in the Channel and poor intelligence, combined with Edward's own inability to make up his mind. Edward did not board his flagship until the end of August, nearly four months after the date originally envisaged. His fleet was then pinned to the coast by adverse winds for six weeks.

By the end of September 1372, French armies had overrun the whole of Poitou and most of Saintonge and the county of Angoulême. The nobility of Poitou had agreed a truce with their invaders. Under its terms, the province was to transfer its allegiance back to the King of France unless Edward or the Black Prince appeared with an army at Thouars in northern Poitou by the end of November. Meanwhile, the English fleet had got no further than the Sussex port of Winchelsea. Edward's ministers decided to abandon the campaign. On 5 October, the Black Prince came before a packed meeting of the royal council at Westminster, bearing the charters investing him with the principality of Aquitaine and resigned all of his continental titles and possessions into his father's hands. The bulk of the fleet was paid off on the following day. Edward himself seems to have had little part in these decisions, and for a time refused to accept them. Confined to his quarters on board the *Grace Dieu* off the Sussex coast, he would not disembark for another week. At Thouars, the nobility of Poitou submitted to Charles V of France. Almost all the territories ceded to Edward III at Brétigny had now been lost.

The defeats of 1372 marked the end of his active role in government. The dominant place in the conduct of the war now passed to John of Gaunt and to William Latimer and his friends. Enjoying neither the legitimacy of the king nor the reputation of the Prince of Wales, they were widely regarded as chancers out for themselves. Gaunt had married Constance, the eldest daughter of the dead King Pedro of Castile in 1371, and had assumed the title of King of Castile. He was determined to divert the English war effort towards making his claim a reality. But the disastrous outcome of his 800-mile march from Calais to Bordeaux in 1373, in which most of his army was claimed by exhaustion, exposure and disease without fighting a single battle or siege, discredited him as a soldier. The councillors who remained at home lined their own pockets at the king's expense. They acquired crown lands and leases at low prices. They lent money to the king on highly favourable terms. A number of them were engaged in trading in royal wardships and crown leases, or bought up old, dishonoured debt at a heavy discount and used their influence in government to get it paid at face value. Latimer, Alice Perrers and the London financier Richard Lyons were the main beneficiaries of these schemes.

In the spring of 1374, John of Gaunt abandoned his campaigns in south-western France for want of funds and reinforcements from England, and returned to a glacial reception at home. Shorn of its most productive provinces, Aquitaine was now no longer economically or militarily self-supporting. With the decline of the English merchant marine, the province was beyond the reach of English armies; and a bankrupt English state was no longer capable of supporting it financially. As a result, it was left to fend for itself. No further cash subsidies were sent to Aquitaine. No major English expeditionary army fought there again until 1412. Year after year, the French launched campaigns up the valleys of the Garonne and the Dordogne towards Bordeaux, eating further into the shrinking territory under English control. The same pattern was repeated elsewhere. Brittany was progressively reoccupied by the French crown, leaving John de Montfort a refugee in England and Brest the only remaining stronghold under English control. The fortress of Saint-Sauveur, England's last outpost in Normandy, surrendered after a long siege in 1375. Portugal and Flanders, England's only significant continental allies, moved into the orbit of France. At the end of June 1375, after several months of negotiation, a truce was sealed at Bruges for an initial period of a year. Its terms effectively acknowledged that Edward had lost. With extensions, it remained in force for the rest of his reign.

On 28 April 1376, the 'Good Parliament', one of the most famous parliaments of the medieval period, opened at Westminster. For the next ten weeks, the storm of anger and frustration provoked by seven years of ineffective government and military defeat broke over the heads of Edward's ministers. The terms of the truce of Bruges were regarded as a humiliation, and John of Gaunt, its chief English architect, was blamed for it. Edward III's former triumphs came back to haunt his ministers. To the Commons, which did not understand the exceptional conditions in which the English had prevailed in the 1350s, there seemed to be no explanation for recent failures other than treachery and folly. They mounted a sustained attack on the king's government, discreetly encouraged from his sickbed by the Black Prince. Latimer and Lyons were impeached. Alice Perrers was forbidden by statute to appear within the confines of the royal court, on pain of losing all her assets.

When the Good Parliament was dissolved on 10 July 1376, Edward was not strong enough to receive the Commons' petitions, as tradition dictated. They were obliged to send a delegation before him at the royal manor of Eltham. It was a dismal occasion. The Commons declined to vote a subsidy. Edward for his part declined to act on their petitions. It was the last notable public occasion of the old king's career. In the remaining months of his father's life, John of Gaunt made it his business to reverse the humiliations of the Good Parliament. The leaders of the parliamentary opposition were hounded. William of Wykeham, who five years after his dismissal had returned in the unlikely guise of a prominent opponent of the court, was deprived of his assets. The Speaker of the House of Commons was imprisoned for contempt. Latimer, Lyons and Alice Perrers returned to court, and received royal pardons.

The Black Prince, who had died at Kennington in the last weeks of the Parliament, was splendidly interred beside the high altar of Canterbury Cathedral early in October 1376. 'On his death,' wrote the chronicler Thomas Walsingham, 'the hopes of England utterly perished.'[4] Edward III was not present at his son's funeral. He was now barely capable of attending to public affairs for more than short stretches. His small court moved at irregular intervals between the royal manors around London, keeping to the shadows, out of sight of his subjects. We have some vivid glimpses of his life in these pathetic final weeks: a hooded barge rowed slowly up the Thames bearing the prostrate king from Havering to Sheen while Londoners crowded round in small boats hoping for a final glimpse of him; the chamberlain, standing guard outside his chamber and quarrelling with petitioners trying to get in; the king coming to the door to find out what the noise was about, and taking the documents out of the petitioners hands; the occasional formal audiences with ministers, the old man propped up on his chair with cushions, looking blankly ahead as Alice Perrers stood by defiantly. Making a supreme effort, the old king had himself rowed to Windsor for the Garter festivities of St George's Day 1377, the fiftieth anniversary year of his accession. In the last great pageant of his reign, he knighted his grandson Richard of Bordeaux, the son of the Black Prince and heir to the throne. The heirs of many of the major noble houses of England received knighthoods on the same occasion, leaders of a new generation destined to participate in the divisions and defeats of the next reign.

On 21 June 1377, the king suffered a serious stroke at the royal manor of Sheen. Paralysed and speechless, he declined rapidly and died in the early hours of the morning. According to the malicious chronicler Thomas Walsingham, in his last moments he was attended by only a single priest. The men-at-arms of his household had already slipped away to ingratiate themselves with the new regime. Alice Perrers was reported to have fled the scene, taking the rings from his fingers as she went. The truce with France had just three days to run. Within ten days of the old king's death, Castilian galleys would be cruising off the south coast and French troops would be fighting in the ruins of Rye, while armies gathered in Scotland and on the march of Aquitaine to complete the destruction of Edward's work.

'Here lies the glory of England, the paragon of past kings, the model of future ones . . . the unconquered leopard,' ran the obituary commissioned by his successor for his tomb in Westminster Abbey.[5] These conventional pieties mocked Edward's final years. If he had been cut off in his prime, like Henry V half a century later, he would perhaps have been the 'unconquered leopard'. But he lived too long, and ended his life a heroic failure. He outlived his own mental and physical powers, the closest companions of his wars, his greatest ministers and lieutenants, and his heir. But the truth was that his ambitions were not frustrated by the failure of his powers or the inadequacy of his last ministers. They were frustrated by their own contradictions. Without any significant measure of support among the French, Edward had set out to overcome a country with several times the resources of his own. He had achieved spectacular victories in the field and in the conference chamber. But the Treaty of Brétigny, which marked the high point of his achievement, could never have represented a permanent settlement. The circumstances which produced it were too extraordinary. So Edward was condemned to see thirty years of conquests reversed in less than five. After a lifetime devoted to conquest in Scotland and France, he ended his reign with precisely the territory that he had started with. He died leaving his realm exhausted by intensive taxation and persistent military failure. He had healed the bitter divisions which he had inherited from his father, but bequeathed others to his successor, Richard II, which would one day contribute to his destruction.

Notes

In quotations from primary sources, translations are usually my own, even where there is an English translation in the edition cited.

1. EDWARD OF WINDSOR (1312–1330)

1. Jean Froissart, *Chroniques de Jean Froissart*, ed. S. Luce, G. Raynaud, L. and A. Mirot, 15 vols (Paris: Société de l'Histoire de France, 1869–1975), I, p. 215.
2. H. G. Richardson and G. O. Sayles, *The Governance of Mediaeval England from the Conquest to Magna Carta* (Edinburgh: Edinburgh University Press, 1963), App. VII, p. 467.
3. Lord Cooper of Culross, 'The Declaration of Arbroath Revisited', in *Selected Papers 1922–1954* (Edinburgh: Oliver & Boyd, 1957), p. 333.
4. Quoted in J. G. Black, 'Edward I and Gascony in 1300', *English Historical Review*, XVII (1902), pp. 518, 523.
5. *Foedera, Conventiones, Literae et Acta Publica*, ed. T. Rymer, 7 vols (London: 1826–69), II, p. 631.
6. *Foedera*, II, p. 650.
7. Adam Murimuth, *Adae Murimuth Continuatio Chronicarum*, ed. E. M. Thompson (London: Eyre & Spottiswoode, 1889), p. 68.
8. Sir Thomas Gray, *Scalacronica (1272–1363)*, ed. A. King (Woodbridge: Boydell Press for the Surtees Society, 2005), p. 104.
9. Geoffrey Baker, *Chronicon Galfridi le Baker de Synebroke*, ed. E. M. Thompson (Oxford: Oxford University Press, 1889), p. 46.

2. THE CHALLENGE OF WAR (1330–1337)

1. Petrarch, *Le familiari*, ed. V. Rossi, 4 vols (Florence: Edizione Nazionale delle Opere di Francesco Petrarca, 1933–42), IV, p. 138 (book XXII, letter 14).
2. Jean le Bel, *Chronique de Jean le Bel*, ed. J. Viard and E. Déprez, 2 vols (Paris: Société de l'Histoire de France, 1904–5), I, pp. 155–6.
3. *Vita Edwardi Secundi*, ed. N. Denholm-Young (London: Nelson, 1957), pp. 55–6.
4. Murimuth, *Continuatio Chronicarum*, p. 68.

5. Andrew of Wyntoun, *The Orygynale Cronykil of Scotland*, ed. D. Laing, 3 vols (Edinburgh: Edmonston and Douglas, 1872–9), II, p. 435.

3. 'KING OF FRANCE' (1337–1347)

1. *Les Grandes Chroniques de France*, ed. J. Viard, 10 vols (Paris: Société de l'Histoire de France, 1920–53), IX, p. 164.
2. *Foedera*, II, p. 1156.
3. *Reports from the Lords' Committees . . . Touching the Dignity of a Peer*, 5 vols (London: 1820–29), V, pp. 27–9.
4. Froissart, *Chroniques*, III, p. 183.

4. PRINCE OF CHIVALRY (1347–1360)

1. Henry Knighton, *Knighton's Chronicle 1337–1396*, ed. and trans. G. H. Martin (Oxford: Clarendon Press, 1995), pp. 150–51.
2. *Foedera*, III, pp. 340–41.
3. Froissart, *Chroniques*, VI, p. 4.

5. DECLINE AND FALL (1360–1377)

1. E. Perroy, 'Charles V et le traité de Brétigny', *Le Moyen Age*, 2nd series, XXIX (1928), p. 266.
2. Gontier de Bagneux, in R. Delachenal, *Histoire de Charles V*, 5 vols (Paris: Alphonse Picard & Fils, 1909–31), III, pp. 551–3.
3. Froissart, *Chroniques*, VI, p. 80.
4. Thomas Walsingham, *The St Albans Chronicle: The Chronica Maiora of Thomas Walsingham*, ed. J. Taylor, W. Childs and L. Watkiss, 2 vols (Oxford: Oxford University Press, 2003–11), I, p. 36.
5. *Inventory of the Historical Monuments of London*, vol. I, *Westminster Abbey* (London: HMSO, 1924), p. 30.

Further Reading

The best modern biography is W. M. Ormrod's *Edward III* (New Haven, Conn.: Yale University Press, 2011), an outstanding work of modern Edwardian scholarship by an author who devoted his career to the study of the period. Clifford J. Rogers, *War Cruel and Sharp: English Strategy under Edward III, 1327–1360* (Woodbridge: Boydell Press, 2000), is the fullest account of Edward as a strategist and commander. Both works are inclined to attribute to foresight decisions which I would put down to accident or fortune, but it is a defensible view. The first three volumes of my own *The Hundred Years War – Trial by Battle, Trial by Fire* and *Divided Houses* (London: Faber & Faber, 1990–2009) – cover diplomacy and war on both sides of the Channel. An excellent abridged translation of Froissart's *Chronicles* by Geoffrey Brereton has been published in Penguin Classics (Harmondsworth: Penguin, 1978). For all the chronicler's inaccuracies, no other contemporary source conveys such a vivid feel for the period.

Edward's leading captains are well covered by the *Oxford Dictionary of National Biography*. More detailed biographies include Kenneth Fowler, *The King's Lieutenant: Henry of Grosmont, First Duke of Lancaster, 1310–1361* (London: Elek, 1969), and Anthony Goodman, *John of Gaunt* (Harlow: Longman, 1992), although the older biography by Sydney Armitage-Smith, *John of Gaunt* (London: Constable, 1904), is still worth reading. There is no entirely satisfactory life of the Black Prince, but Richard Barber, *Edward, Prince of Wales and Aquitaine* (Woodbridge: Boydell Press, 1978), and David Green, *Edward, the Black Prince* (Harlow: Longman, 2007), are both valuable.

For individual campaigns, see Ranald Nicholson, *Edward III and the Scots* (Oxford: Oxford University Press, 1965); Andrew Ayton and Philip Preston, *The Battle of Crécy, 1346* (Woodbridge: Boydell Press, 2005); H. J. Hewitt, *The Black Prince's Expedition of 1355–1357* (Manchester: Manchester University Press, 1958); and David Green's less detailed but more reflective *The Battle of Poitiers, 1356* (Stroud: Tempus, 2002). For all things Iberian, including the Nájera campaign, the fundamental work is P. E. Russell, *The English Intervention in Spain and Portugal in the Time of Edward III and Richard II* (Oxford: Clarendon Press, 1955). The crisis of Edward III's dotage is admirably covered by George Holmes, *The Good Parliament* (Oxford: Clarendon Press, 1975).

There are many excellent books on aspects of late medieval civilization which are central to an understanding of Edward III's life. Maurice Keen, *The Laws of War in the Late Middle Ages* (London: Routledge & Kegan Paul, 1965), is a revelatory study by a fine scholar, far broader than its title might suggest. On chivalry, an inexhaustible subject, see the same author's fundamental *Chivalry* (New Haven, Conn.: Yale University Press, 1984) and Nigel Saul, *For Honour and Fame: Chivalry in England, 1066–1500* (London: Bodley Head, 2011). Barbara W. Tuchman, *A Distant Mirror: The Calamitous 14th Century* (London: Macmillan, 1978), is a colourful and perceptive account of Edward III's world, seen through the life of the French paladin Enguerrand de Coucy.

Picture Credits

1. Edward III doing homage to Philip VI of France at Amiens, 1329. Miniature from the *Grandes Chroniques de France*, fourteenth century (Bibliothèque de l'Arsenal, Paris/Photo12/Getty Images)
2. Declaration of war sent by Edward III to Philip VI in July 1340 (Archives Nationales, Paris, inv. AEIII67)
3. The Battle of Sluys, 24 June 1340. Miniature from Jean Froissart's *Chronicles*, fourteenth century (Bibliothèque Nationale, Paris/Getty Images)
4. Edward III's gold noble, obverse showing the king on a ship, Calais mint, 1344 (Fitzwilliam Museum, University of Cambridge/Bridgeman Images)
5. The English army crossing the Seine in 1346. Miniature from the *Chroniques de France ou de St Denis*, fourteenth century (British Library, London/Bridgeman Images)
6. The Battle of Crécy, 26 August 1346. Miniature from Jean Froissart's *Chronicles*, fourteenth century (Bibliothèque Nationale, Paris/Bridgeman Images)
7. Edward III and David, King of Scotland, making peace in 1357. Illuminated initial 'C' from a fourteenth-century English manuscript (British Library, London/The Art Archive)
8. Surrender of the Burghers of Calais to the English army. Miniature from Jean Froissart's *Chronicles*, fourteenth century (Bibliothèque Nationale, Paris/The Art Archive/Alamy)
9. John Constable, *Hadleigh Castle, the Mouth of the Thames: Morning after a Stormy Night*, 1829 (Yale Center for British Art, Paul Mellon Collection/Bridgeman Images)

10. Tomb effigy of Bertrand du Guesclin, marble, fourteenth century (Abbey Church of Saint-Denis/The Art Archive/Manuel Cohen)

11. Tomb effigy of Philippa of Hainault, alabaster, fourteenth century (Westminster Abbey, London/Alamy)

12. Tomb effigy of Edward, the Black Prince, gilt bronze, 1376 (Canterbury Cathedral, Kent/Alamy)

13. Detail of Edward III from the *Great Charter of Liberties*, 1373 (Bristol Museum and Art Gallery/Bridgeman Images)

14. Benjamin West, *The Burghers of Calais* (detail), 1789 (Royal Collection Trust © Her Majesty Queen Elizabeth II, 2016)

Index

Penguin Monarchs

THE HOUSE OF TUDOR

Henry VII	Sean Cunningham
Henry VIII*	John Guy
Edward VI*	Stephen Alford
Mary I*	John Edwards
Elizabeth I	Helen Castor

THE HOUSE OF STUART

James I	Thomas Cogswell
Charles I*	Mark Kishlansky
[Cromwell*	David Horspool]
Charles II*	Clare Jackson
James II	David Womersley
William III & Mary II*	Jonathan Keates
Anne	Richard Hewlings

THE HOUSE OF HANOVER

George I	Tim Blanning
George II	Norman Davies
George III	Amanda Foreman
George IV	Stella Tillyard
William IV	Roger Knight
Victoria*	Jane Ridley

THE HOUSES OF SAXE-COBURG & GOTHA AND WINDSOR

Edward VII*	Richard Davenport-Hines
George V*	David Cannadine
Edward VIII*	Piers Brendon
George VI*	Philip Ziegler
Elizabeth II*	Douglas Hurd

* Now in paperback

ALLEN LANE
an imprint of
PENGUIN BOOKS

Also Published

Jordan B. Peterson, *12 Rules for Life: An Antidote to Chaos*

Bruno Maçães, *The Dawn of Eurasia: On the Trail of the New World Order*

Brock Bastian, *The Other Side of Happiness: Embracing a More Fearless Approach to Living*

Ryan Lavelle, *Cnut: The North Sea King*

Tim Blanning, *George I: The Lucky King*

Thomas Cogswell, *James I: The Phoenix King*

Pete Souza, *Obama, An Intimate Portrait: The Historic Presidency in Photographs*

Robert Dallek, *Franklin D. Roosevelt: A Political Life*

Norman Davies, *Beneath Another Sky: A Global Journey into History*

Ian Black, *Enemies and Neighbours: Arabs and Jews in Palestine and Israel, 1917-2017*

Martin Goodman, *A History of Judaism*

Shami Chakrabarti, *Of Women: In the 21st Century*

Stephen Kotkin, *Stalin, Vol. II: Waiting for Hitler, 1928-1941*

Lindsey Fitzharris, *The Butchering Art: Joseph Lister's Quest to Transform the Grisly World of Victorian Medicine*

Serhii Plokhy, *Lost Kingdom: A History of Russian Nationalism from Ivan the Great to Vladimir Putin*

Mark Mazower, *What You Did Not Tell: A Russian Past and the Journey Home*

Lawrence Freedman, *The Future of War: A History*

Niall Ferguson, *The Square and the Tower: Networks, Hierarchies and the Struggle for Global Power*

Matthew Walker, *Why We Sleep: The New Science of Sleep and Dreams*

Edward O. Wilson, *The Origins of Creativity*

John Bradshaw, *The Animals Among Us: The New Science of Anthropology*

David Cannadine, *Victorious Century: The United Kingdom, 1800-1906*

Leonard Susskind and Art Friedman, *Special Relativity and Classical Field Theory*

Maria Alyokhina, *Riot Days*

Oona A. Hathaway and Scott J. Shapiro, *The Internationalists: And Their Plan to Outlaw War*

Chris Renwick, *Bread for All: The Origins of the Welfare State*

Anne Applebaum, *Red Famine: Stalin's War on Ukraine*

Richard McGregor, *Asia's Reckoning: The Struggle for Global Dominance*

Chris Kraus, *After Kathy Acker: A Biography*

Sayeeda Warsi, *The Enemy Within: A Tale of Muslim Britain*

Alexander Betts and Paul Collier, *Refuge: Transforming a Broken Refugee System*

Robert Bickers, *Out of China: How the Chinese Ended the Era of Western Domination*

Erica Benner, *Be Like the Fox: Machiavelli's Lifelong Quest for Freedom*

William D. Cohan, *Why Wall Street Matters*

David Horspool, *Oliver Cromwell: The Protector*

Daniel C. Dennett, *From Bacteria to Bach and Back: The Evolution of Minds*

Derek Thompson, *Hit Makers: How Things Become Popular*

Harriet Harman, *A Woman's Work*

Wendell Berry, *The World-Ending Fire: The Essential Wendell Berry*

Daniel Levin, *Nothing but a Circus: Misadventures among the Powerful*

Stephen Church, *Henry III: A Simple and God-Fearing King*

Pankaj Mishra, *Age of Anger: A History of the Present*

Graeme Wood, *The Way of the Strangers: Encounters with the Islamic State*

Michael Lewis, *The Undoing Project: A Friendship that Changed the World*

John Romer, *A History of Ancient Egypt, Volume 2: From the Great Pyramid to the Fall of the Middle Kingdom*

Andy King, *Edward I: A New King Arthur?*

Thomas L. Friedman, *Thank You for Being Late: An Optimist's Guide to Thriving in the Age of Accelerations*

John Edwards, *Mary I: The Daughter of Time*

Grayson Perry, *The Descent of Man*

Deyan Sudjic, *The Language of Cities*

Norman Ohler, *Blitzed: Drugs in Nazi Germany*

Carlo Rovelli, *Reality Is Not What It Seems: The Journey to Quantum Gravity*

Catherine Merridale, *Lenin on the Train*

Susan Greenfield, *A Day in the Life of the Brain: The Neuroscience of Consciousness from Dawn Till Dusk*

Christopher Given-Wilson, *Edward II: The Terrors of Kingship*

Emma Jane Kirby, *The Optician of Lampedusa*

Minoo Dinshaw, *Outlandish Knight: The Byzantine Life of Steven Runciman*

Candice Millard, *Hero of the Empire: The Making of Winston Churchill*

Christopher de Hamel, *Meetings with Remarkable Manuscripts*

Brian Cox and Jeff Forshaw, *Universal: A Guide to the Cosmos*

Ryan Avent, *The Wealth of Humans: Work and Its Absence in the Twenty-first Century*

Jodie Archer and Matthew L. Jockers, *The Bestseller Code*

Cathy O'Neil, *Weapons of Math Destruction: How Big Data Increases Inequality and Threatens Democracy*

Peter Wadhams, *A Farewell to Ice: A Report from the Arctic*

Richard J. Evans, *The Pursuit of Power: Europe, 1815-1914*

Anthony Gottlieb, *The Dream of Enlightenment: The Rise of Modern Philosophy*

Marc Morris, *William I: England's Conqueror*

Gareth Stedman Jones, *Karl Marx: Greatness and Illusion*

J.C.H. King, *Blood and Land: The Story of Native North America*

Robert Gerwarth, *The Vanquished: Why the First World War Failed to End, 1917-1923*

Joseph Stiglitz, *The Euro: And Its Threat to Europe*

John Bradshaw and Sarah Ellis, *The Trainable Cat: How to Make Life Happier for You and Your Cat*

A J Pollard, *Edward IV: The Summer King*

Erri de Luca, *The Day Before Happiness*

Diarmaid MacCulloch, *All Things Made New: Writings on the Reformation*

Daniel Beer, *The House of the Dead: Siberian Exile Under the Tsars*

Tom Holland, *Athelstan: The Making of England*

Christopher Goscha, *The Penguin History of Modern Vietnam*

Mark Singer, *Trump and Me*

Roger Scruton, *The Ring of Truth: The Wisdom of Wagner's Ring of the Nibelung*

Ruchir Sharma, *The Rise and Fall of Nations: Ten Rules of Change in the Post-Crisis World*

Jonathan Sumption, *Edward III: A Heroic Failure*

Daniel Todman, *Britain's War: Into Battle, 1937-1941*

Dacher Keltner, *The Power Paradox: How We Gain and Lose Influence*

Tom Gash, *Criminal: The Truth About Why People Do Bad Things*

Brendan Simms, *Britain's Europe: A Thousand Years of Conflict and Cooperation*

Slavoj Žižek, *Against the Double Blackmail: Refugees, Terror, and Other Troubles with the Neighbours*

Lynsey Hanley, *Respectable: The Experience of Class*

Piers Brendon, *Edward VIII: The Uncrowned King*

Matthew Desmond, *Evicted: Poverty and Profit in the American City*

T.M. Devine, *Independence or Union: Scotland's Past and Scotland's Present*

Seamus Murphy, *The Republic*

Jerry Brotton, *This Orient Isle: Elizabethan England and the Islamic World*

Srinath Raghavan, *India's War: The Making of Modern South Asia, 1939-1945*

Clare Jackson, *Charles II: The Star King*

Nandan Nilekani and Viral Shah, *Rebooting India: Realizing a Billion Aspirations*

Sunil Khilnani, *Incarnations: India in 50 Lives*

Helen Pearson, *The Life Project: The Extraordinary Story of Our Ordinary Lives*

Ben Ratliff, *Every Song Ever: Twenty Ways to Listen to Music Now*

Richard Davenport-Hines, *Edward VII: The Cosmopolitan King*

Peter H. Wilson, *The Holy Roman Empire: A Thousand Years of Europe's History*

Todd Rose, *The End of Average: How to Succeed in a World that Values Sameness*

Frank Trentmann, *Empire of Things: How We Became a World of Consumers, from the Fifteenth Century to the Twenty-First*

Laura Ashe, *Richard II: A Brittle Glory*

John Donvan and Caren Zucker, *In a Different Key: The Story of Autism*

Jack Shenker, *The Egyptians: A Radical Story*

Tim Judah, *In Wartime: Stories from Ukraine*

Serhii Plokhy, *The Gates of Europe: A History of Ukraine*

Robin Lane Fox, *Augustine: Conversions and Confessions*

Peter Hennessy and James Jinks, *The Silent Deep: The Royal Navy Submarine Service Since 1945*

Sean McMeekin, *The Ottoman Endgame: War, Revolution and the Making of the Modern Middle East, 1908–1923*

Charles Moore, *Margaret Thatcher: The Authorized Biography, Volume Two: Everything She Wants*

Dominic Sandbrook, *The Great British Dream Factory: The Strange History of Our National Imagination*

Larissa MacFarquhar, *Strangers Drowning: Voyages to the Brink of Moral Extremity*

Niall Ferguson, *Kissinger: 1923-1968: The Idealist*

Carlo Rovelli, *Seven Brief Lessons on Physics*

Tim Blanning, *Frederick the Great: King of Prussia*

Ian Kershaw, *To Hell and Back: Europe, 1914–1949*

Pedro Domingos, *The Master Algorithm: How the Quest for the Ultimate Learning Machine Will Remake Our World*

David Wootton, *The Invention of Science: A New History of the Scientific Revolution*

Christopher Tyerman, *How to Plan a Crusade: Reason and Religious War in the Middle Ages*

Andy Beckett, *Promised You A Miracle: UK 80–82*

Carl Watkins, *Stephen: The Reign of Anarchy*

Anne Curry, *Henry V: From Playboy Prince to Warrior King*

John Gillingham, *William II: The Red King*

Roger Knight, *William IV: A King at Sea*

Douglas Hurd, *Elizabeth II: The Steadfast*

Richard Nisbett, *Mindware: Tools for Smart Thinking*

Jochen Bleicken, *Augustus: The Biography*

Paul Mason, *PostCapitalism: A Guide to Our Future*

Frank Wilczek, *A Beautiful Question: Finding Nature's Deep Design*

Roberto Saviano, *Zero Zero Zero*

Owen Hatherley, *Landscapes of Communism: A History Through Buildings*

César Hidalgo, *Why Information Grows: The Evolution of Order, from Atoms to Economies*

Aziz Ansari and Eric Klinenberg, *Modern Romance: An Investigation*

Sudhir Hazareesingh, *How the French Think: An Affectionate Portrait of an Intellectual People*

Steven D. Levitt and Stephen J. Dubner, *When to Rob a Bank: A Rogue Economist's Guide to the World*

Leonard Mlodinow, *The Upright Thinkers: The Human Journey from Living in Trees to Understanding the Cosmos*

Hans Ulrich Obrist, *Lives of the Artists, Lives of the Architects*

Richard H. Thaler, *Misbehaving: The Making of Behavioural Economics*

Sheldon Solomon, Jeff Greenberg and Tom Pyszczynski, *Worm at the Core: On the Role of Death in Life*

Nathaniel Popper, *Digital Gold: The Untold Story of Bitcoin*

Dominic Lieven, *Towards the Flame: Empire, War and the End of Tsarist Russia*

Noel Malcolm, *Agents of Empire: Knights, Corsairs, Jesuits and Spies in the Sixteenth-Century Mediterranean World*

James Rebanks, *The Shepherd's Life: A Tale of the Lake District*

David Brooks, *The Road to Character*

Joseph Stiglitz, *The Great Divide*

Ken Robinson and Lou Aronica, *Creative Schools: Revolutionizing Education from the Ground Up*

Clotaire Rapaille and Andrés Roemer, *Move UP: Why Some Cultures Advances While Others Don't*

Jonathan Keates, *William III and Mary II: Partners in Revolution*

David Womersley, *James II: The Last Catholic King*

Richard Barber, *Henry II: A Prince Among Princes*

Jane Ridley, *Victoria: Queen, Matriarch, Empress*

John Gray, *The Soul of the Marionette: A Short Enquiry into Human Freedom*

Emily Wilson, *Seneca: A Life*